France
Coloring Book

Adult Coloring Books

Aryla Publishing 2020

978-1-912675-86-9

www.arylapublishing.com

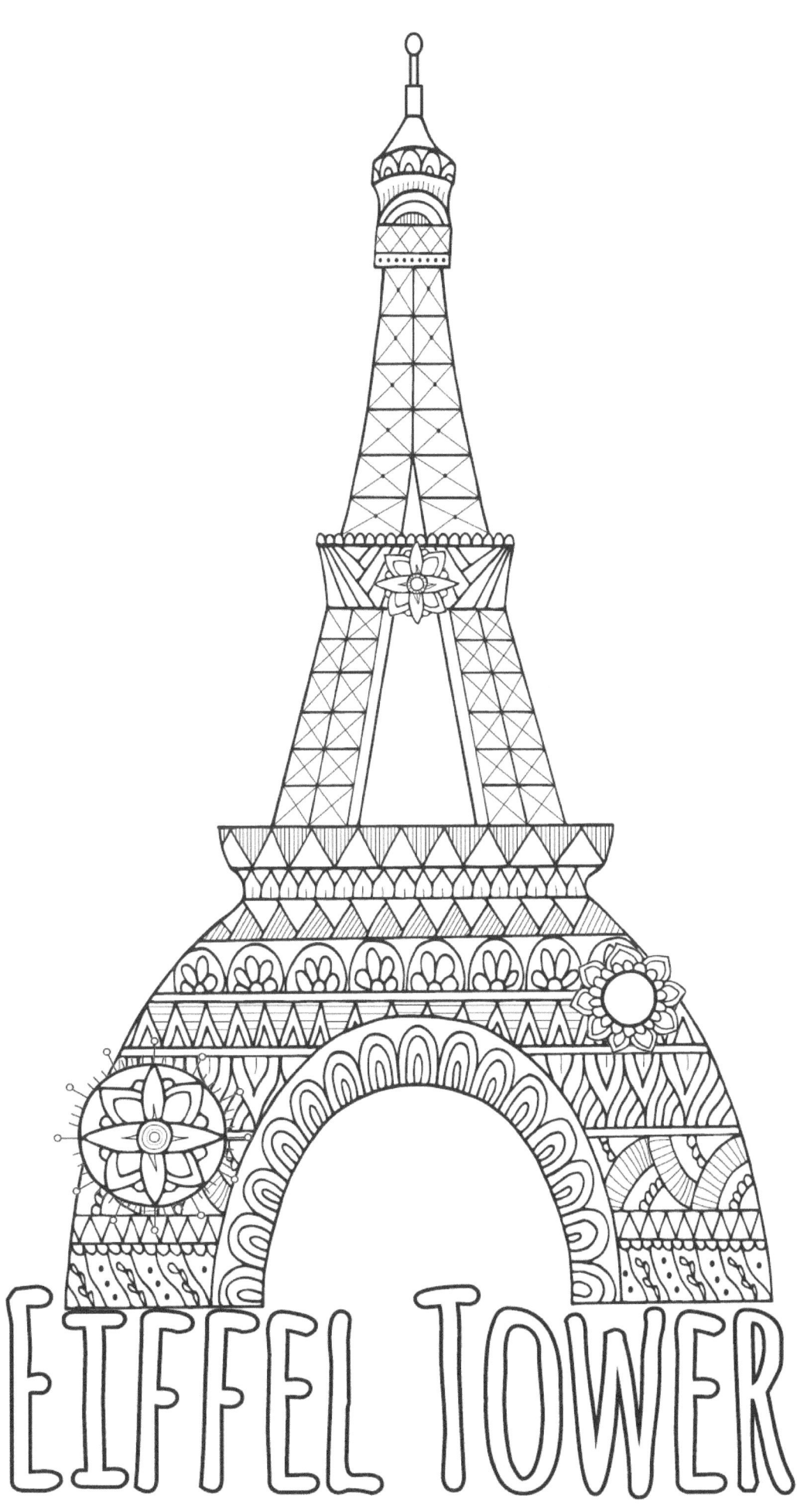

EIFFEL TOWER

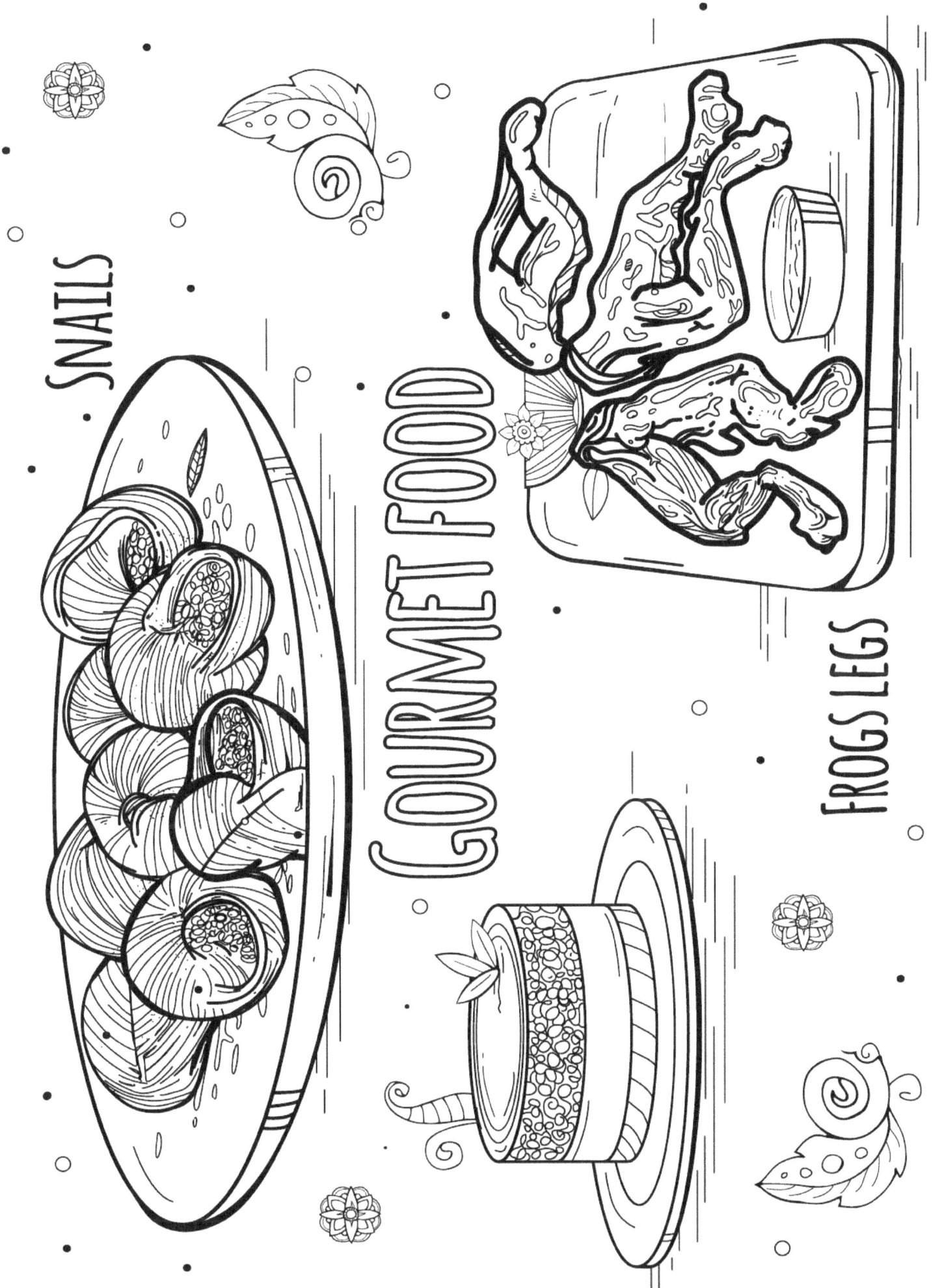

SNAILS

GOURMET FOOD

FROGS LEGS

FRENCH ART

CLAUDE MONET

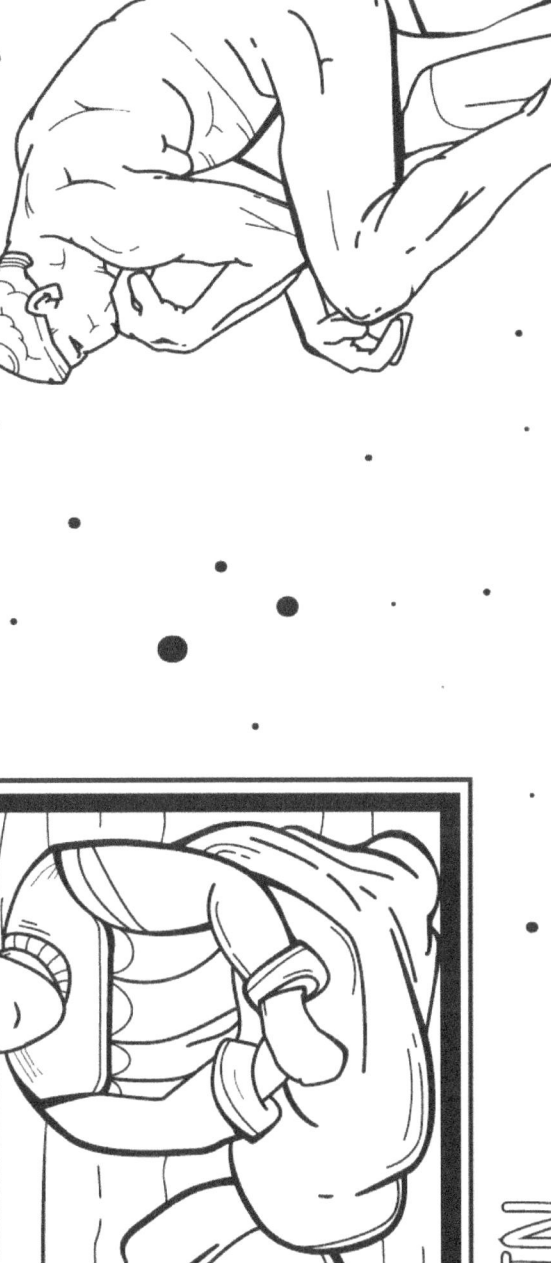

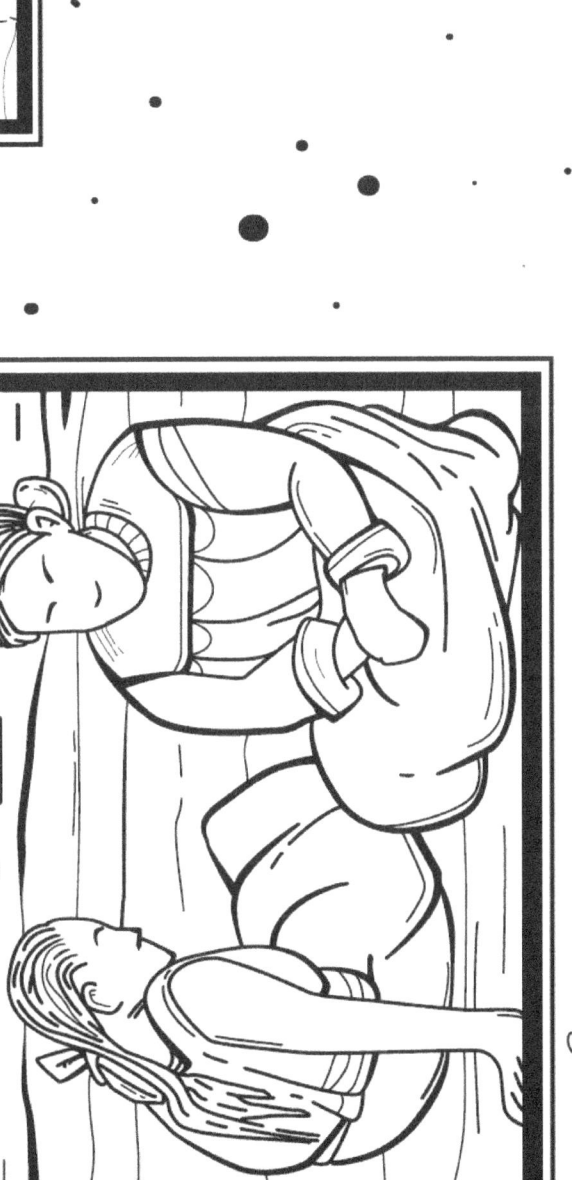

SCULPTURE BY AUGUSTE RODIN

PAUL GAUGUIN

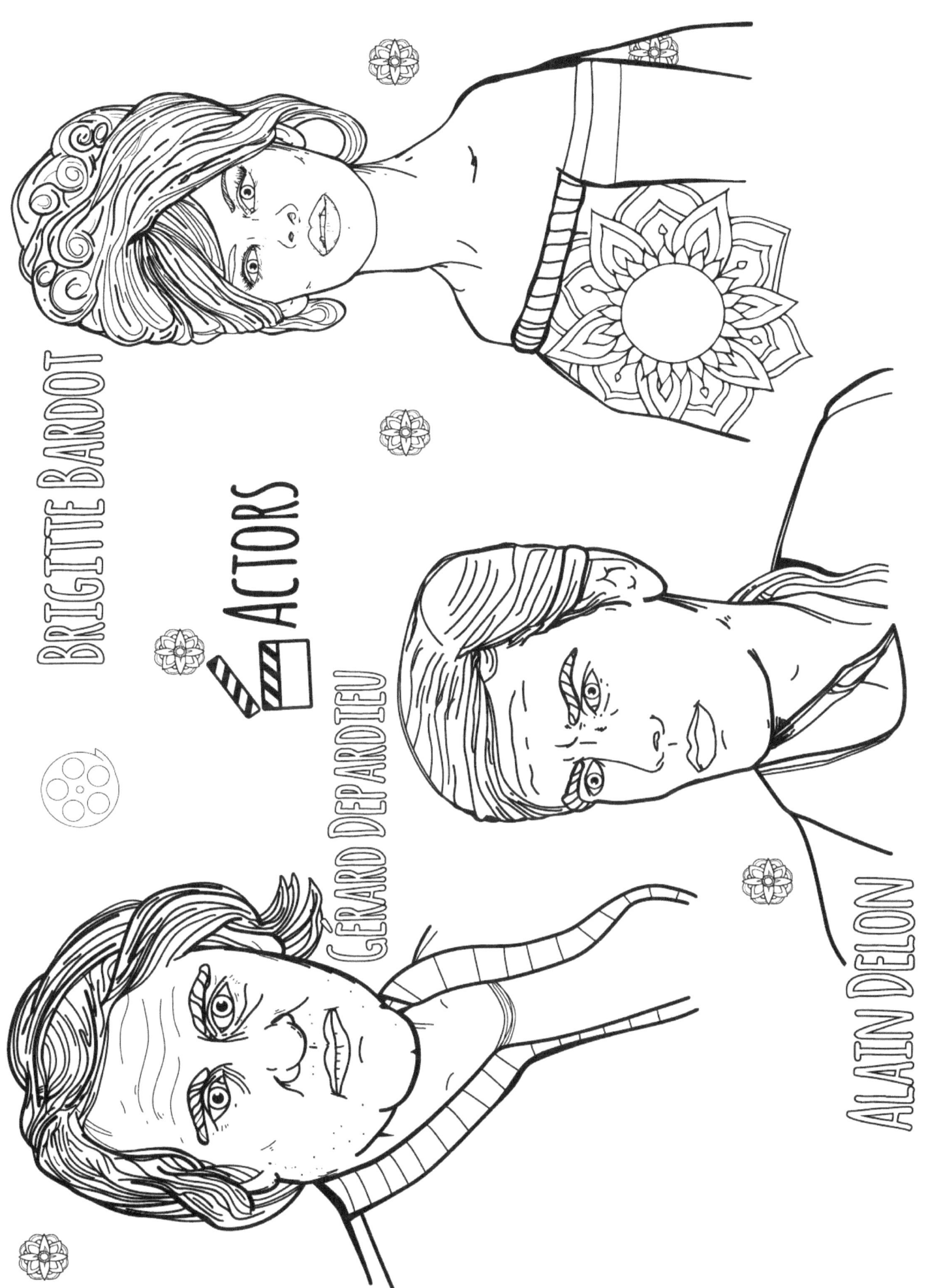

BRIGITTE BARDOT

ACTORS

GÉRARD DEPARDIEU

ALAIN DELON

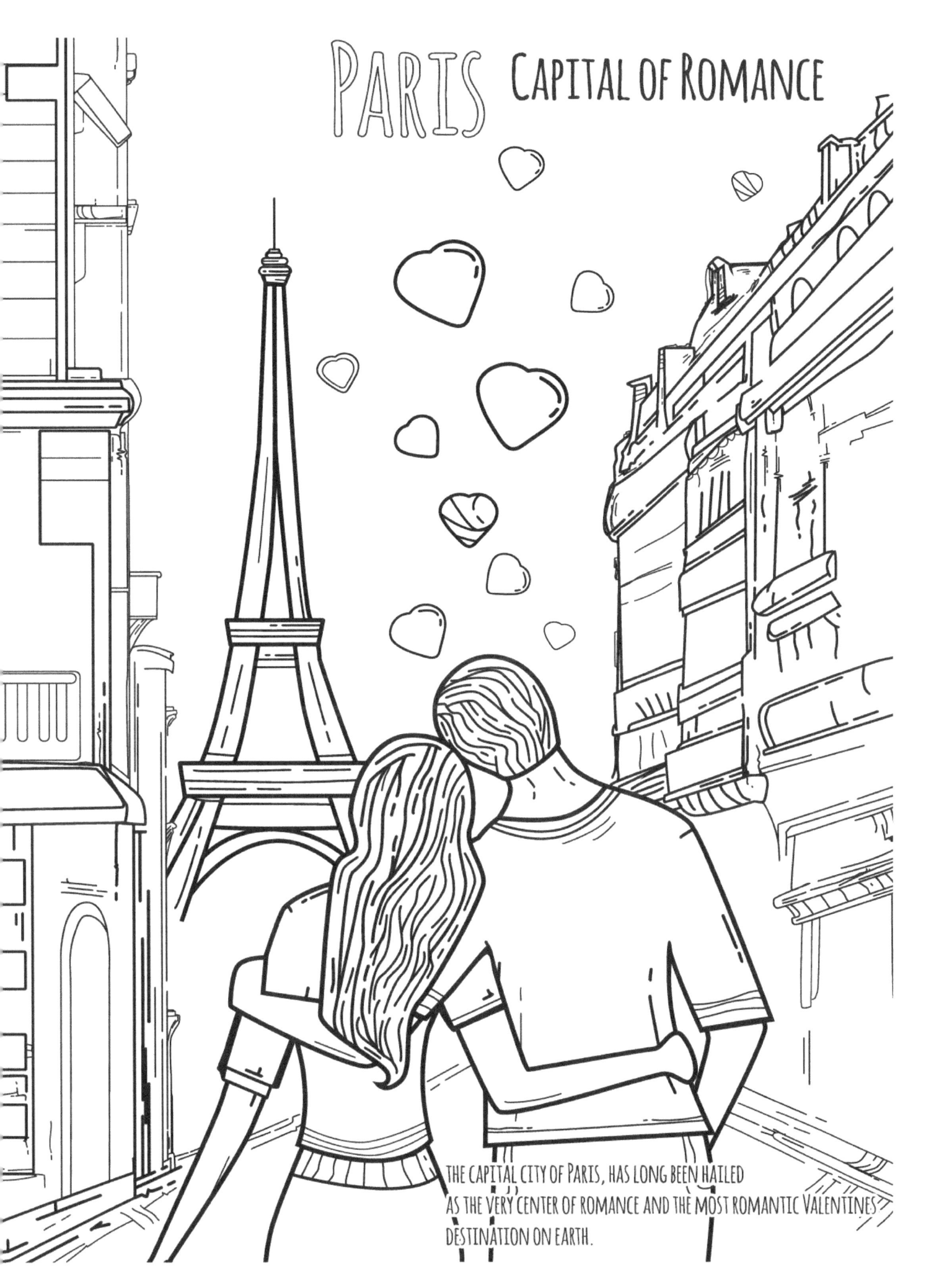

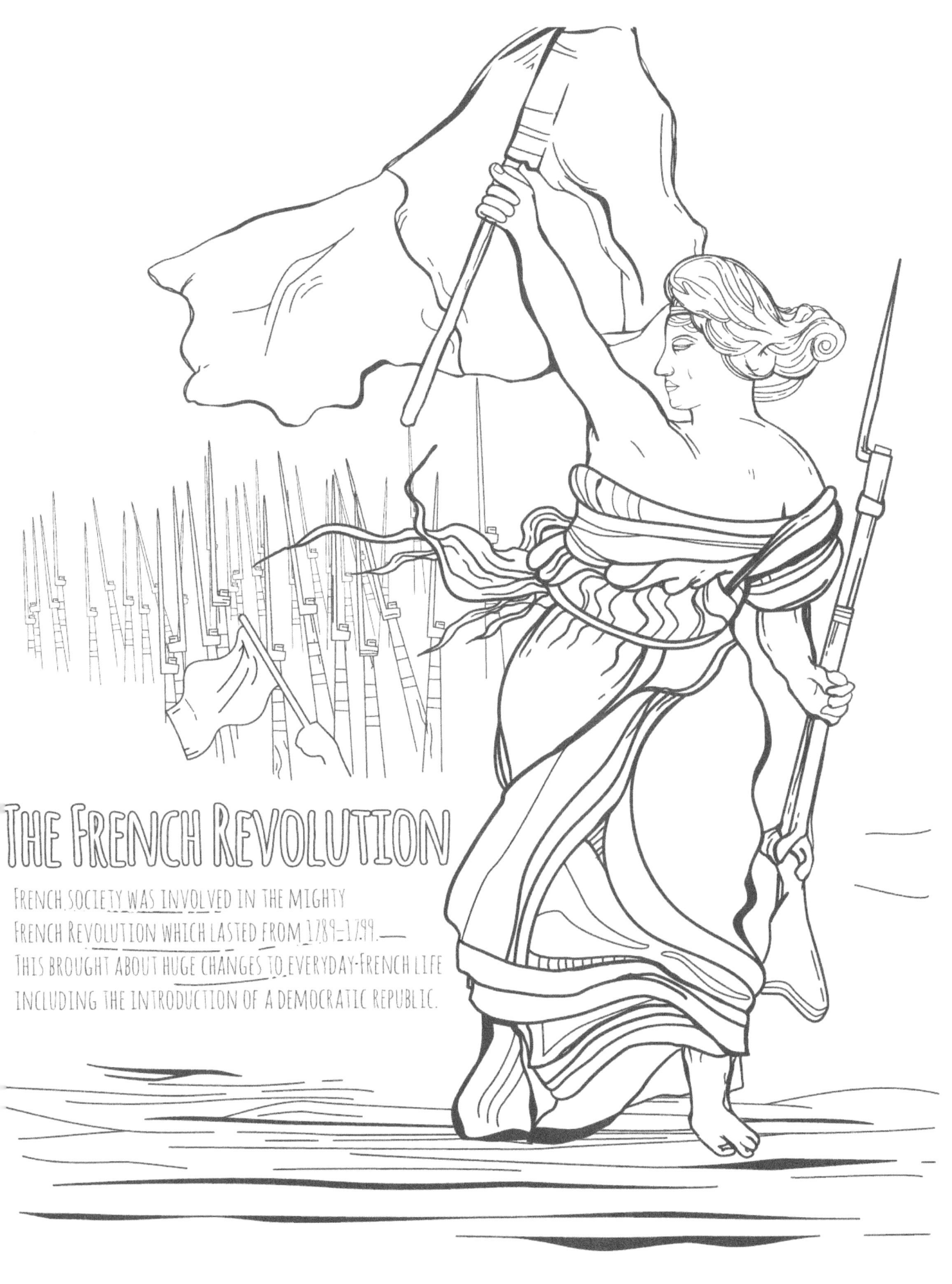

The French Revolution

French society was involved in the mighty
French Revolution which lasted from 1789-1799.
This brought about huge changes to everyday French life
including the introduction of a democratic republic.

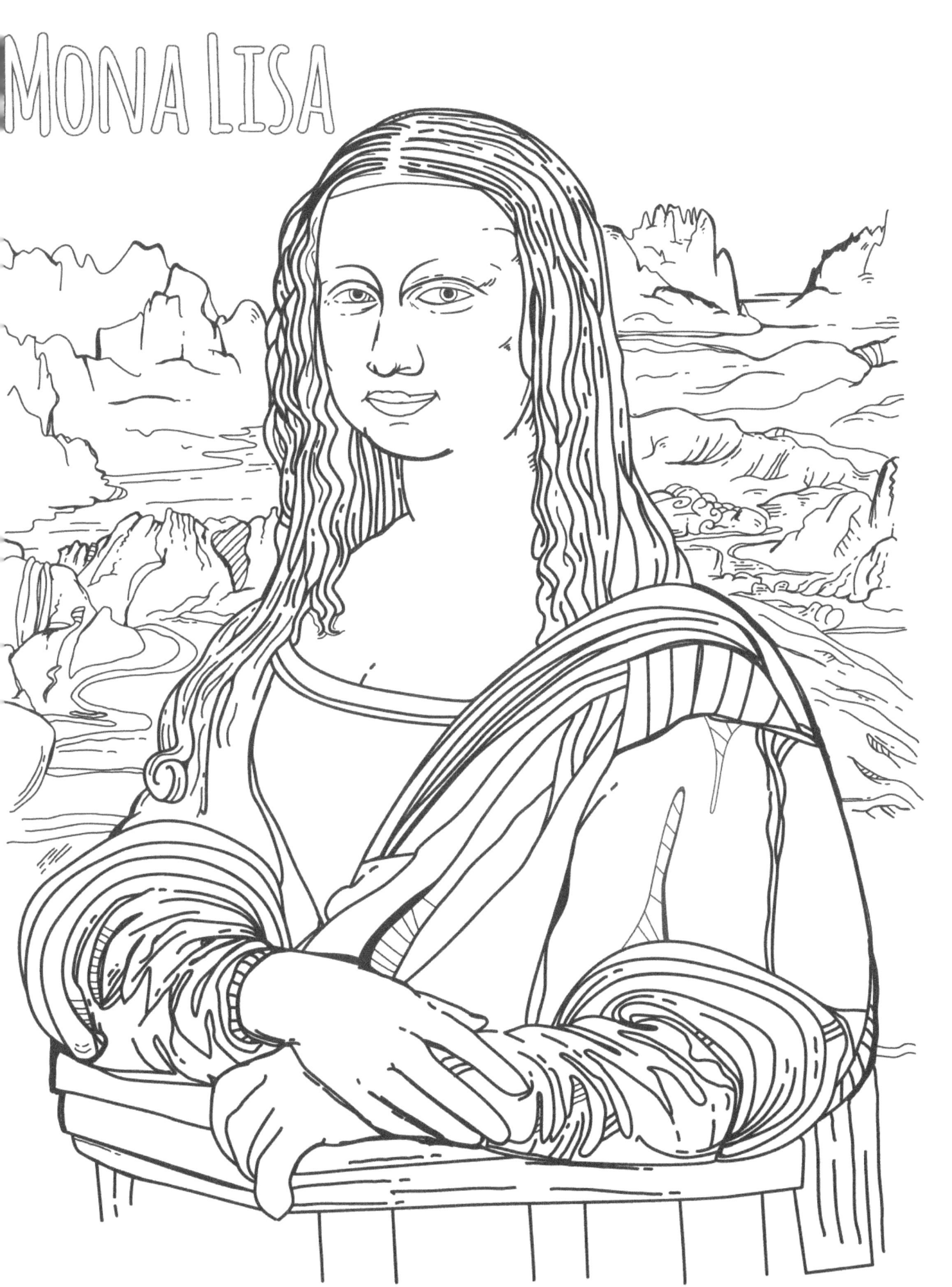

MONA LISA

LES MISERABLES

THE MOST FAMOUS THEATRE SHOW IN HISTORY, WHICH IS NOW ALSO A SMASH-HIT MOVIE, IS SET IN FRANCE AT THE TIME OF THE FRENCH REVOLUTION.

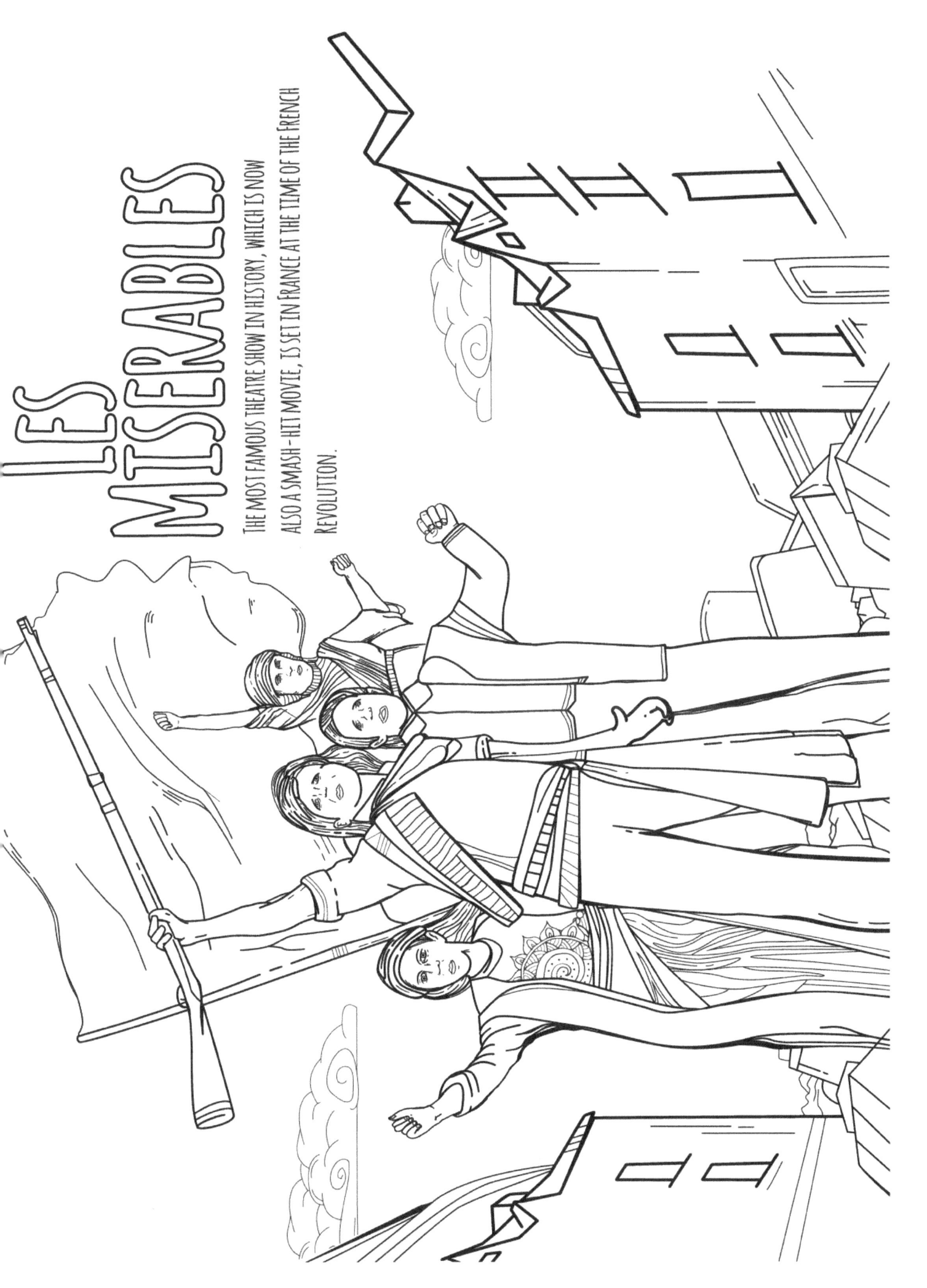

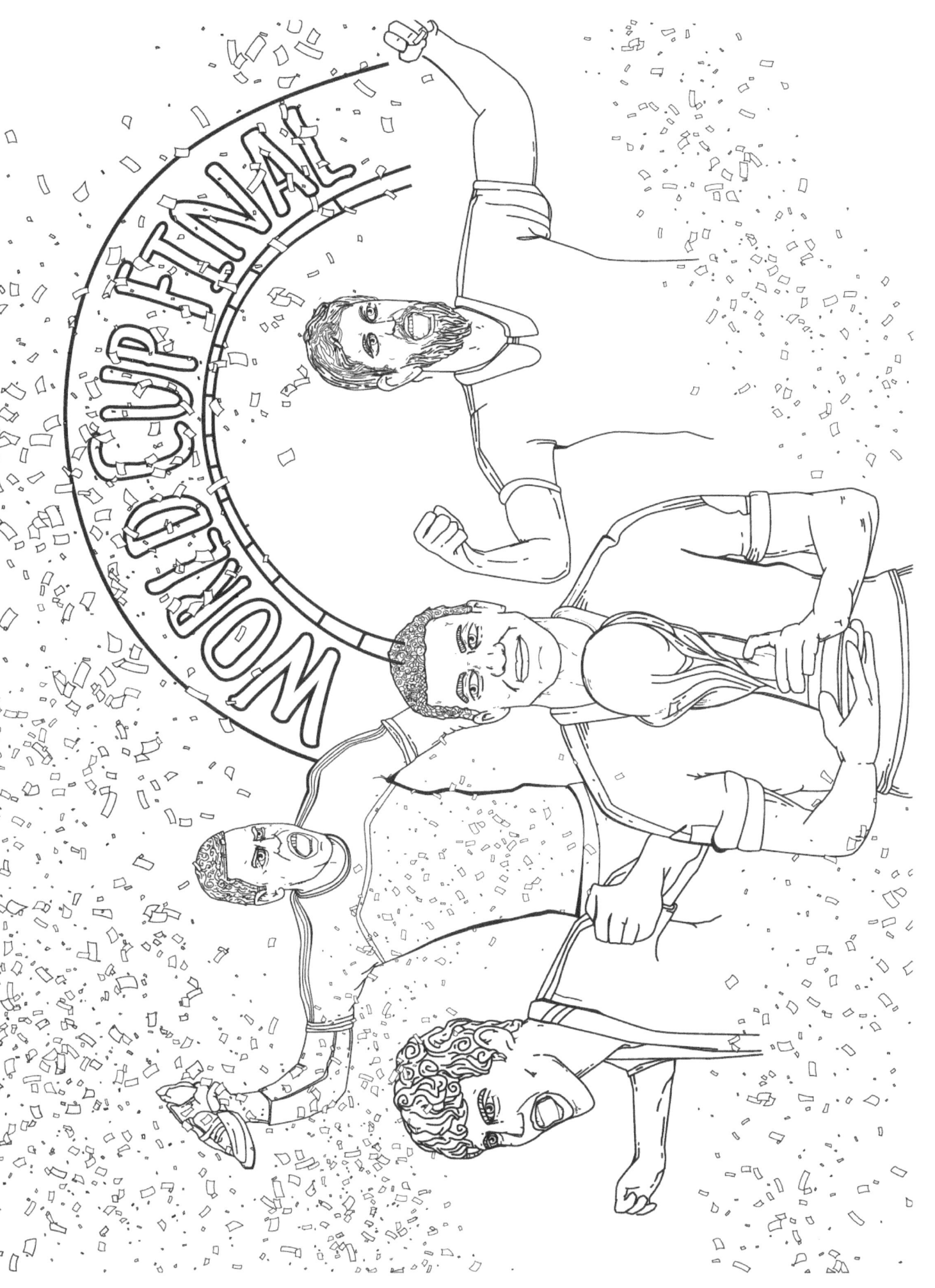

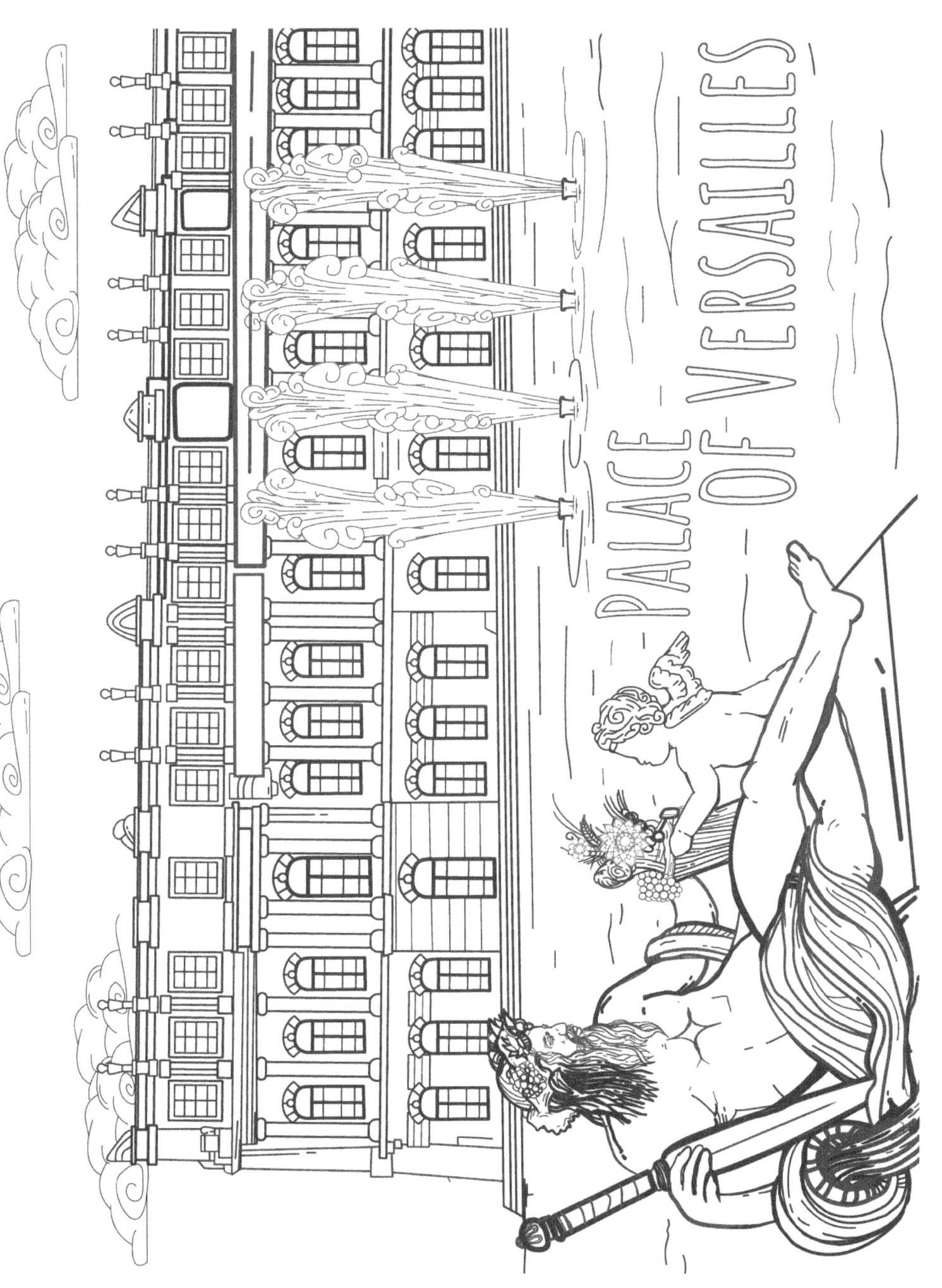

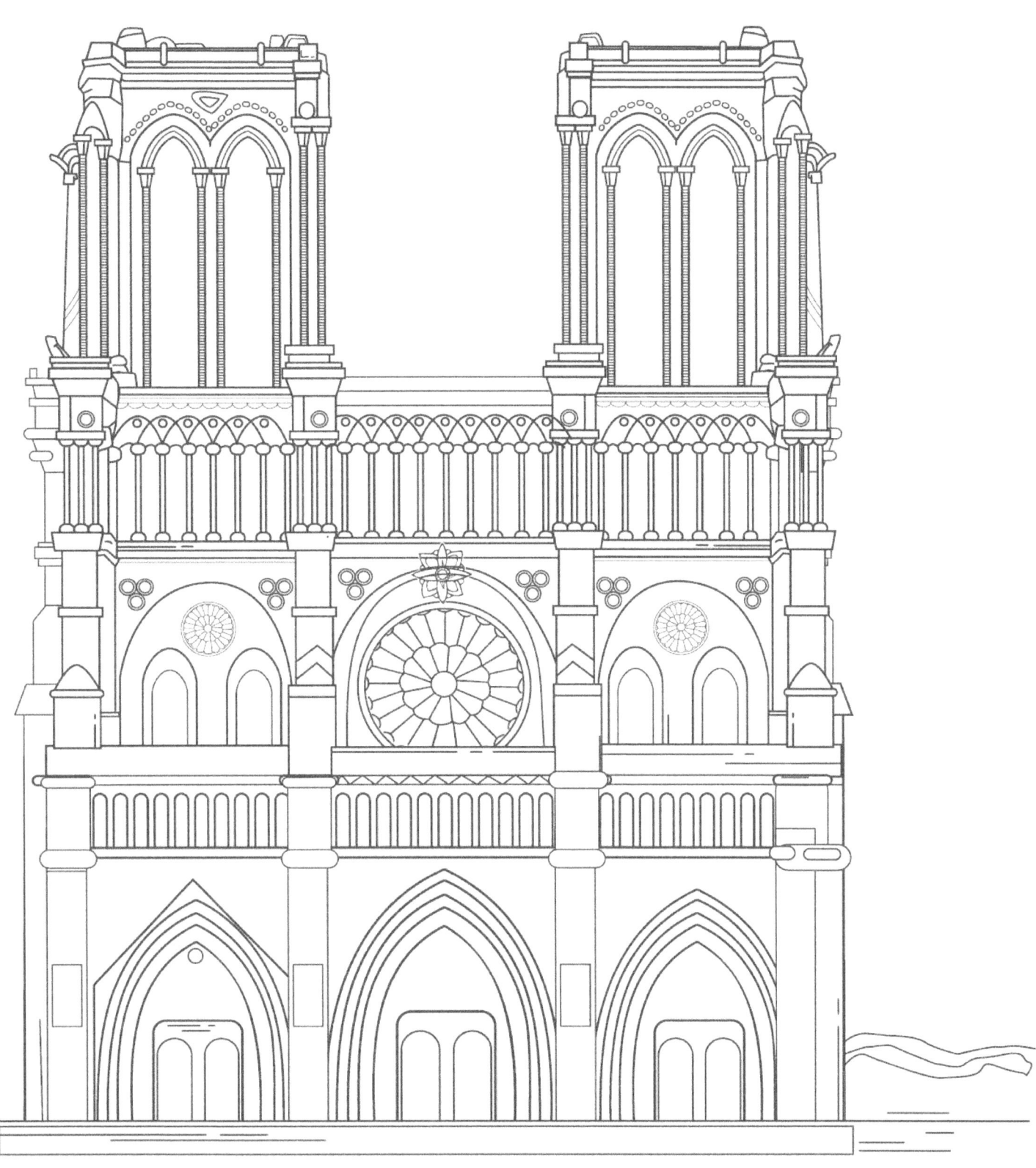

Notre Dame Cathedral

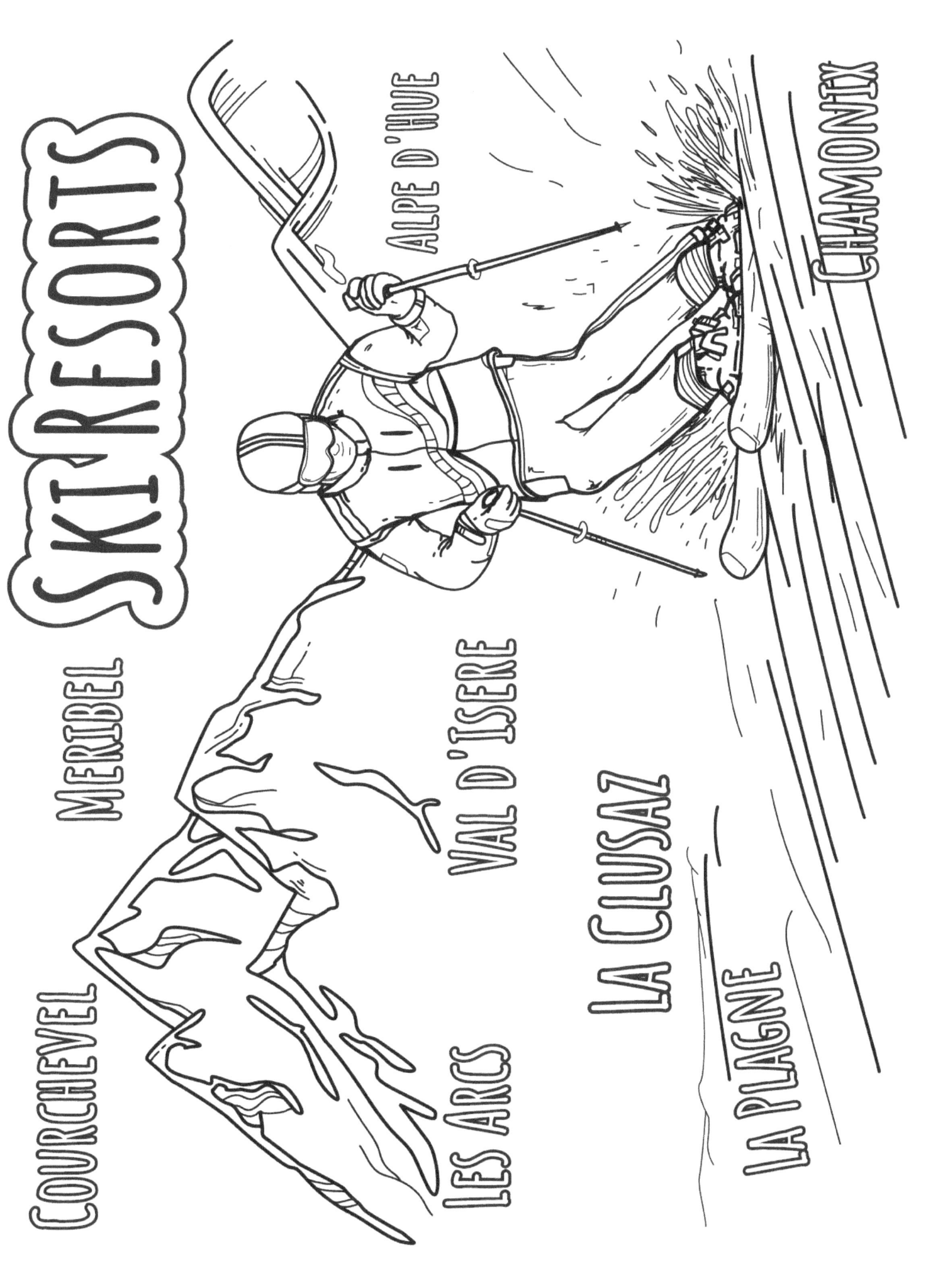

SKI RESORTS

COURCHEVEL

MERIBEL

ALPE D'HUE

CHAMONIX

LES ARCS

VAL D'ISERE

LA CLUSAZ

LA PLAGNE

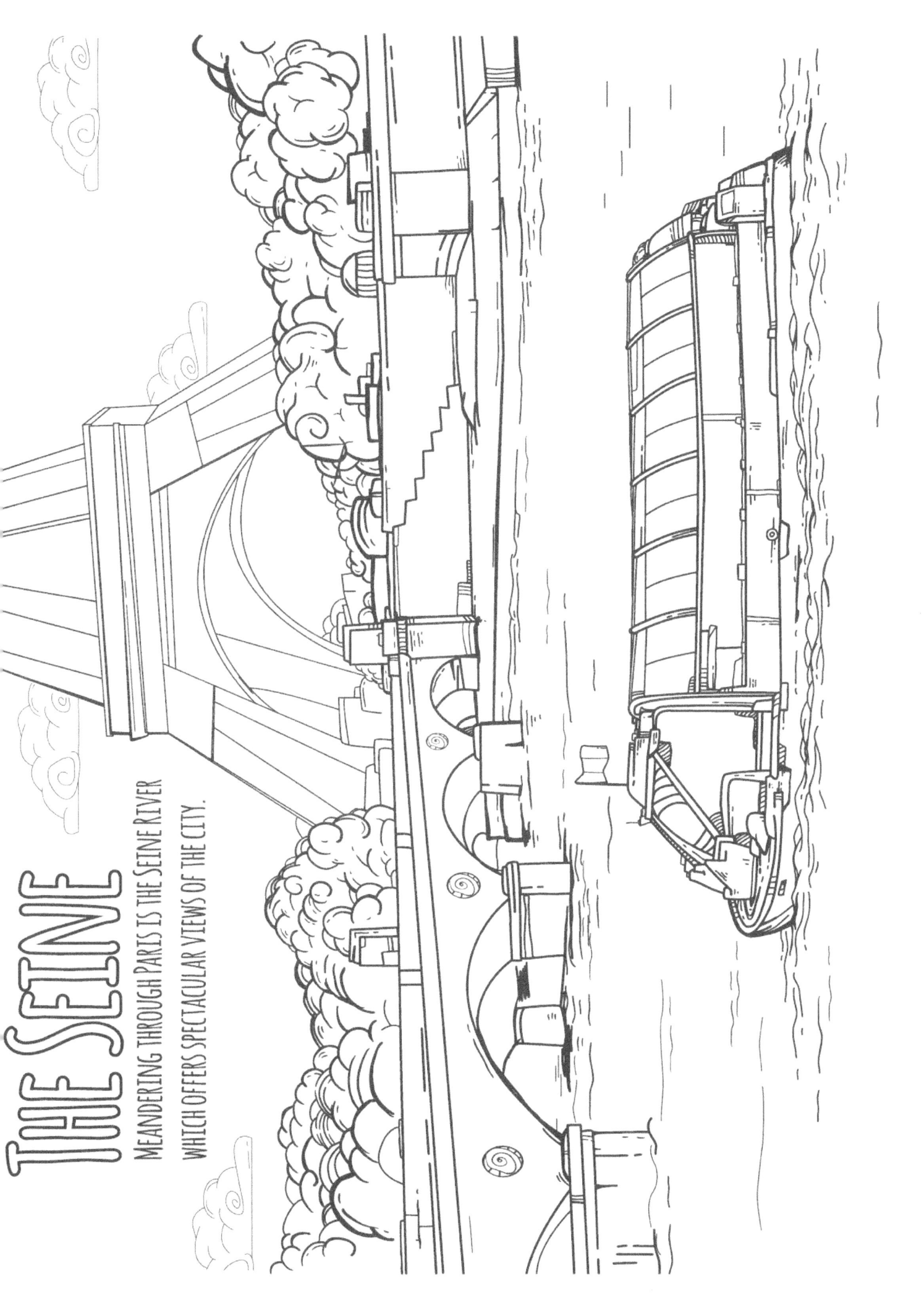

THE SEINE

MEANDERING THROUGH PARIS IS THE SEINE RIVER WHICH OFFERS SPECTACULAR VIEWS OF THE CITY.

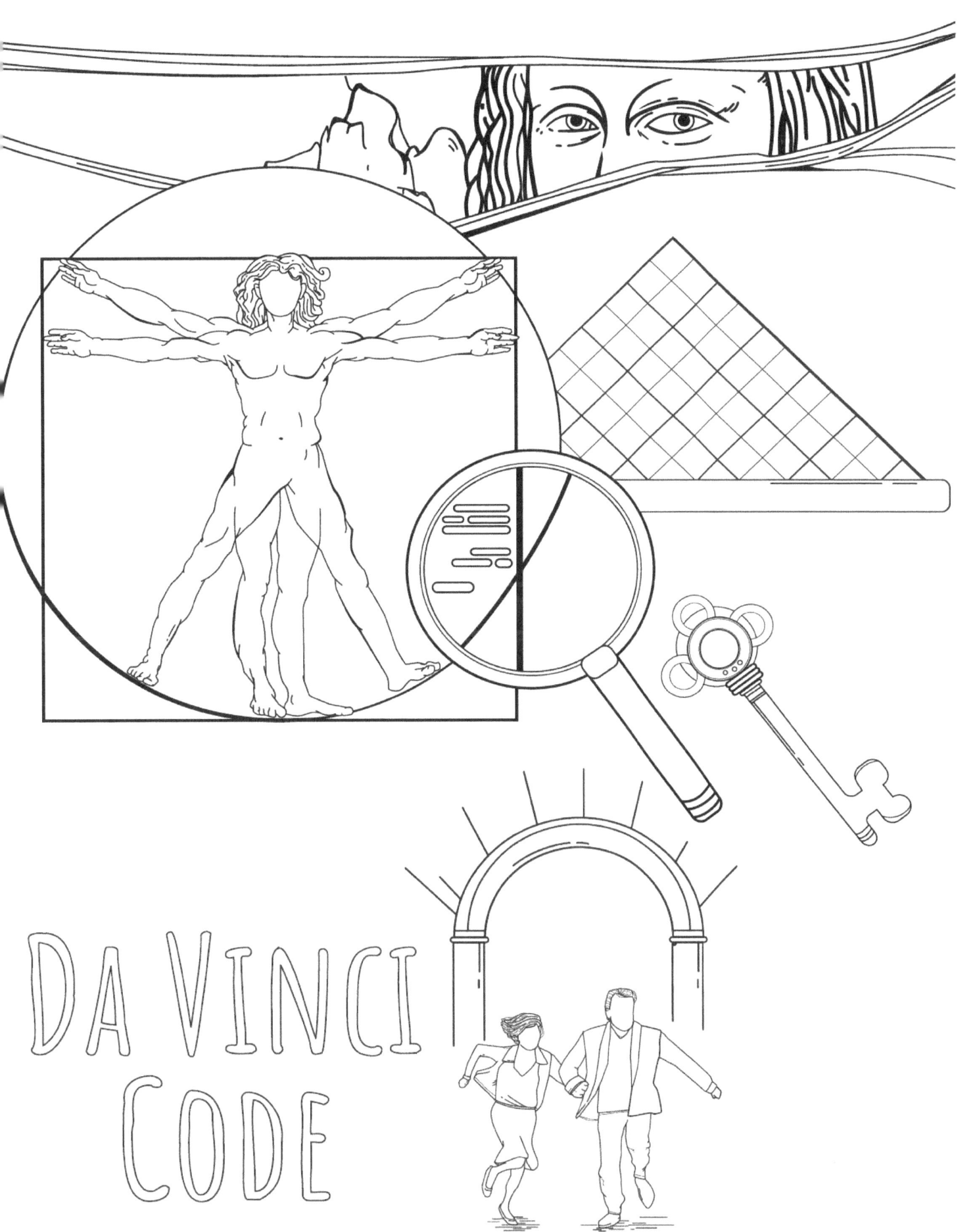

DA VINCI CODE

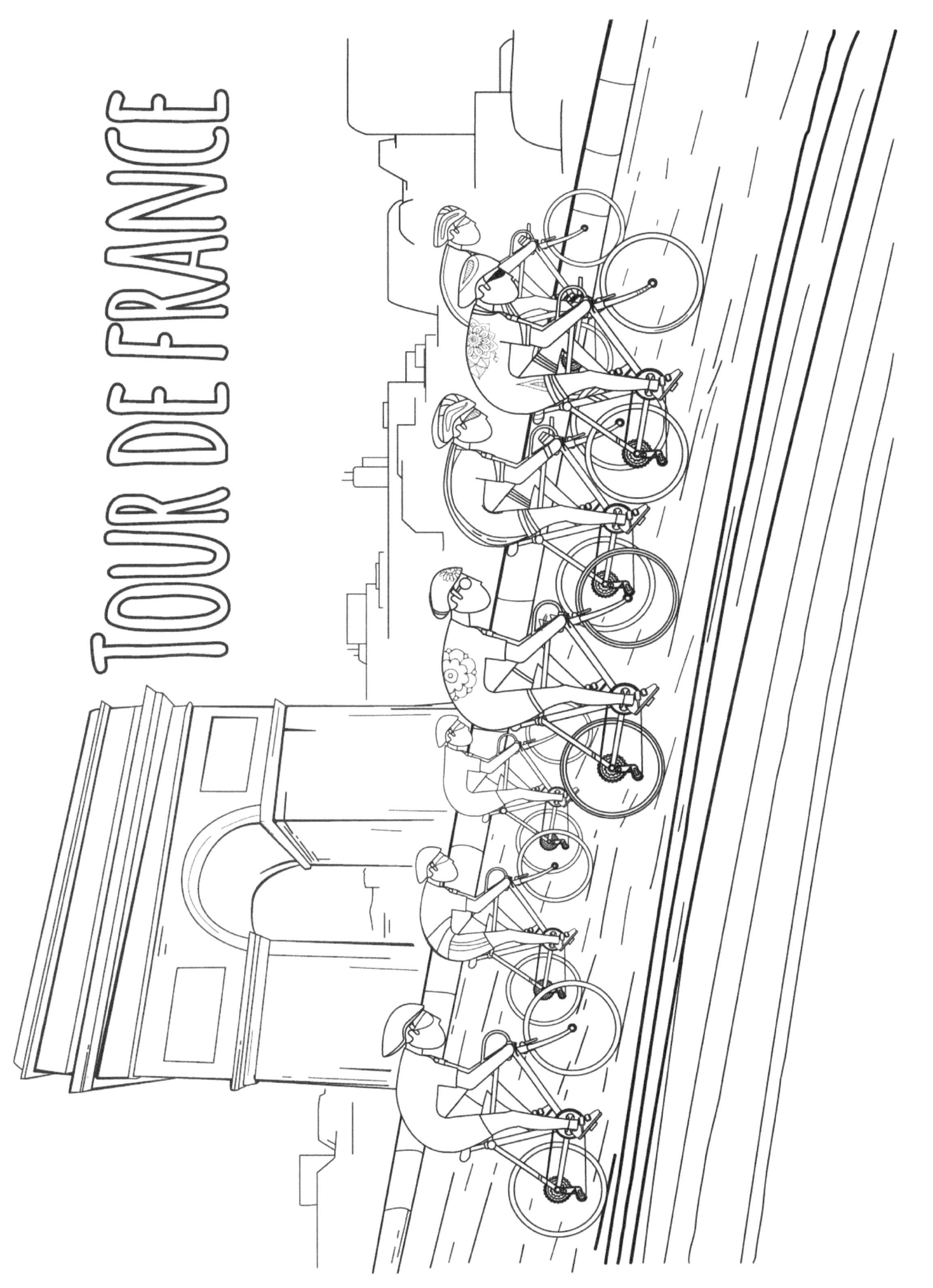

MONACO

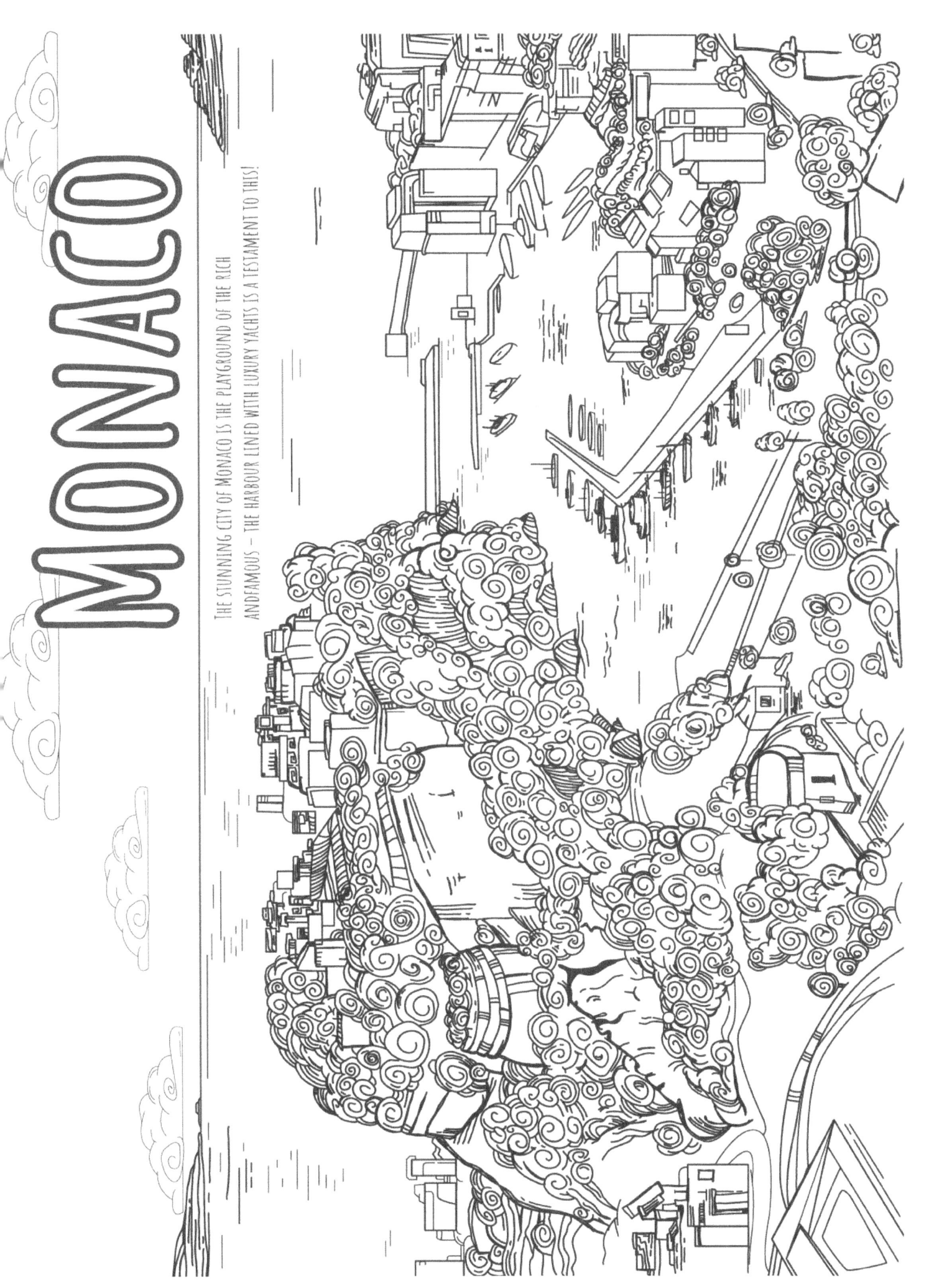

THE STUNNING CITY OF MONACO IS THE PLAYGROUND OF THE RICH AND FAMOUS — THE HARBOUR LINED WITH LUXURY YACHTS IS A TESTAMENT TO THIS!

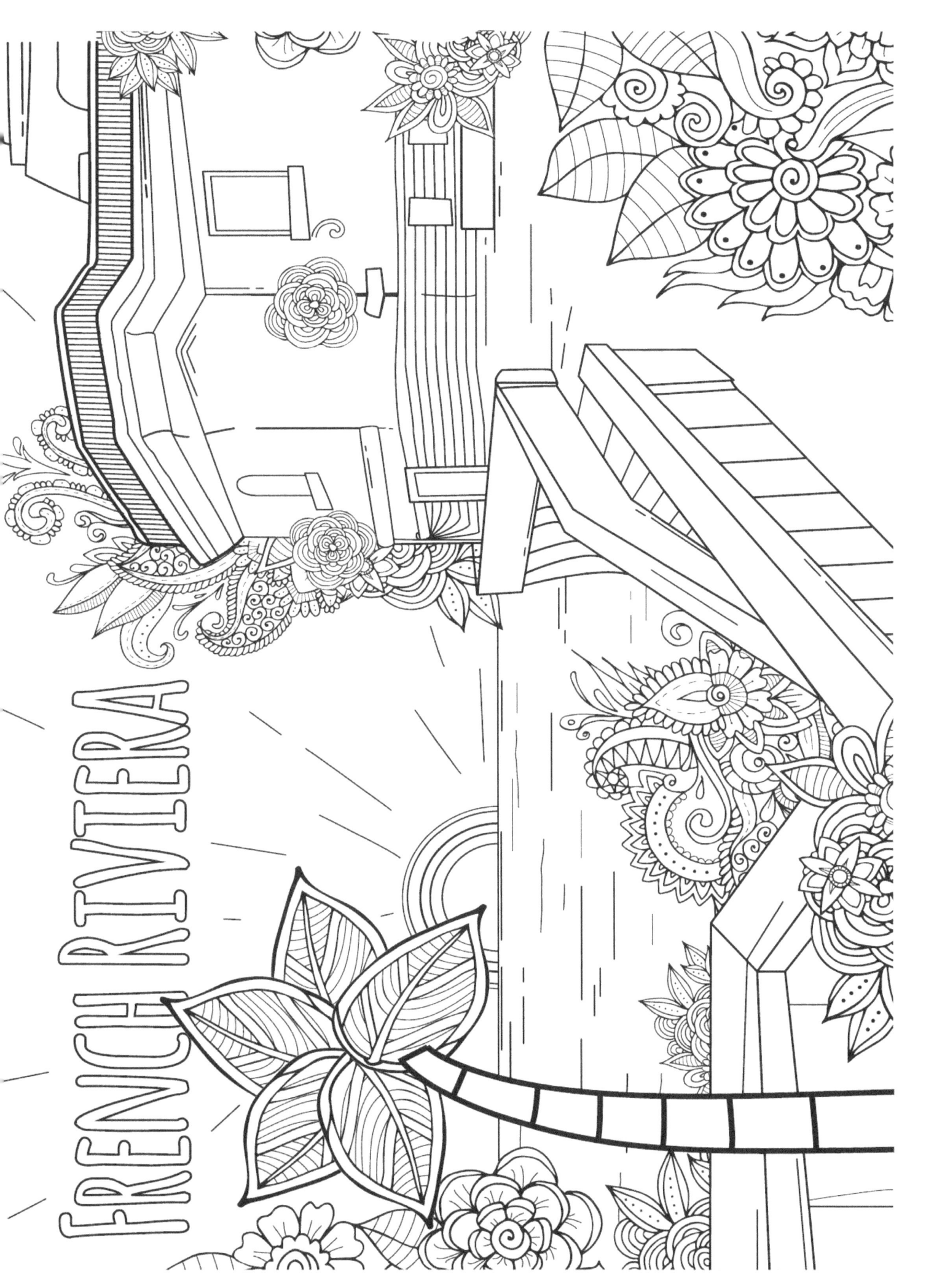

Highest Mountain in Europe- Mont Blanc in the Alps is the tallest mountain within Europe and is popular with skiiers. French Alps

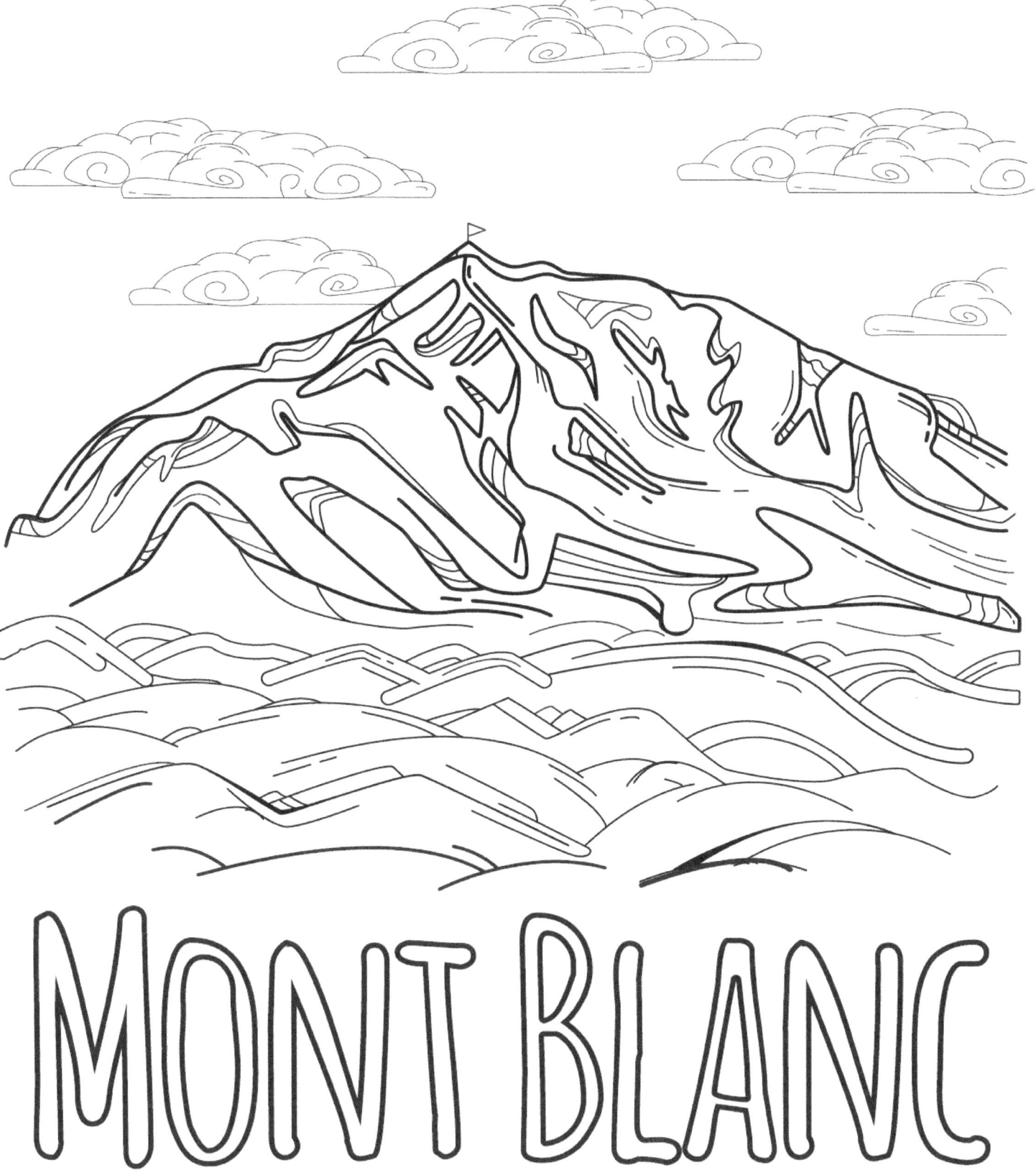

MONT BLANC

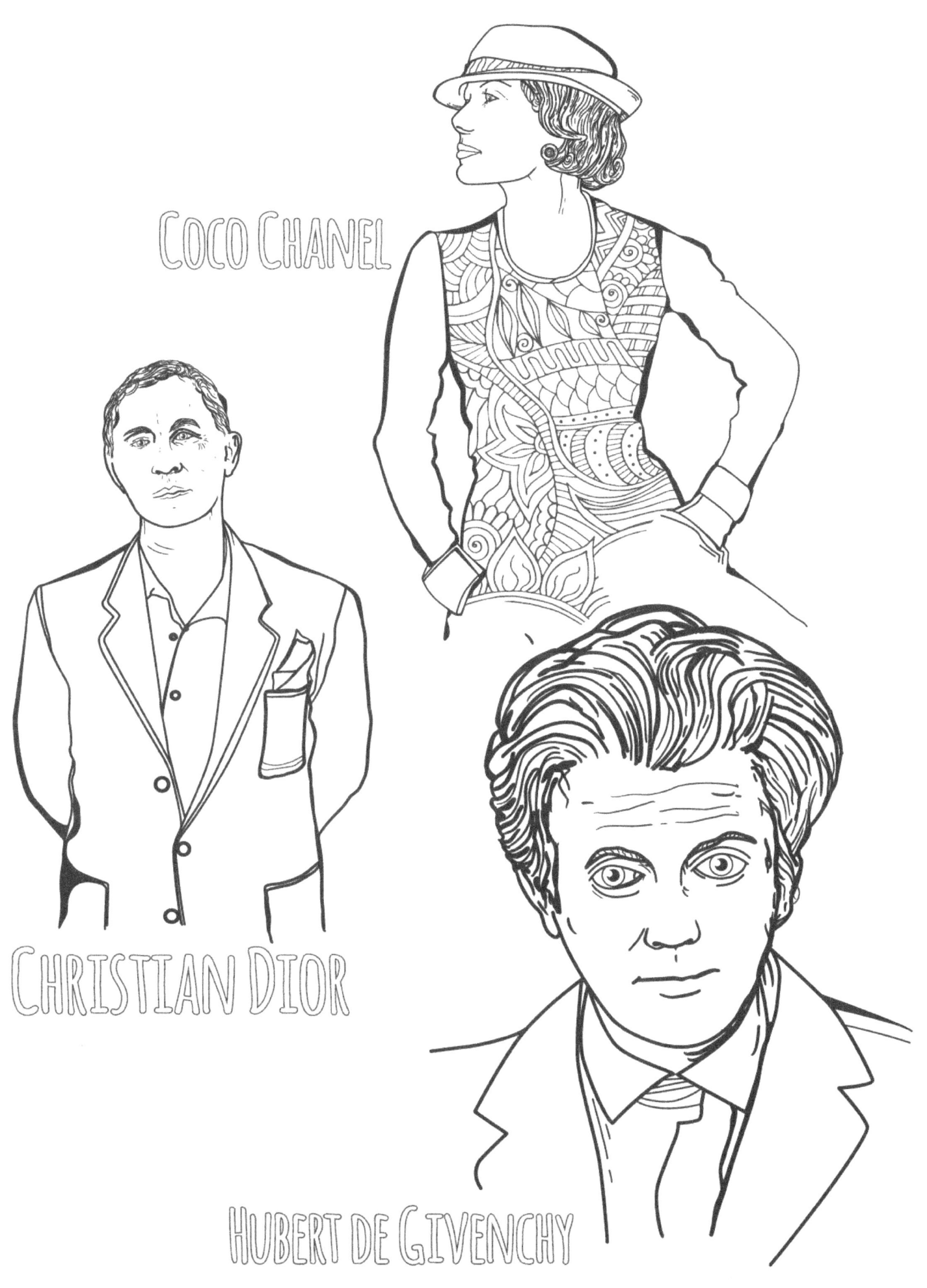

Coco Chanel

Christian Dior

Hubert de Givenchy

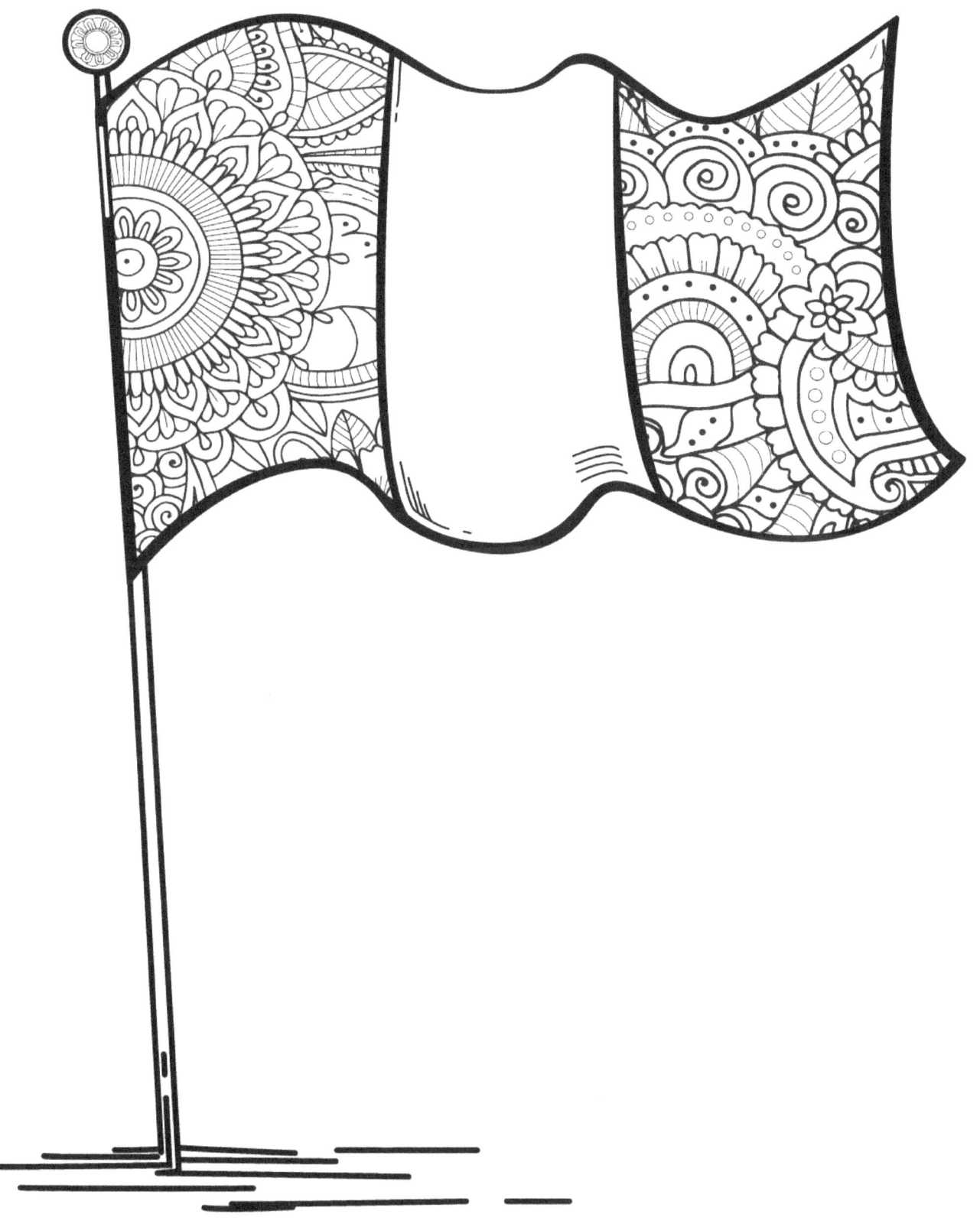

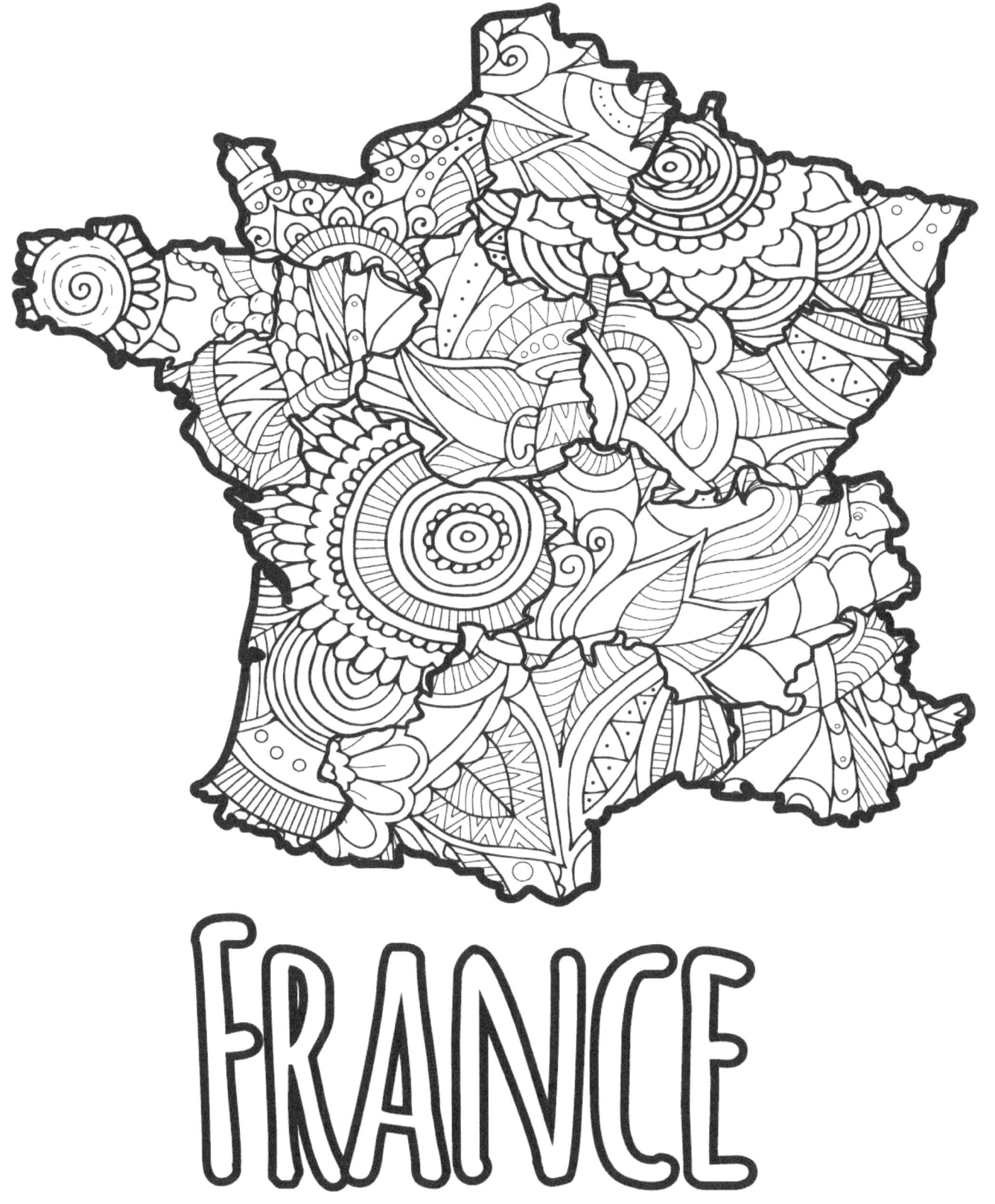

FRANCE

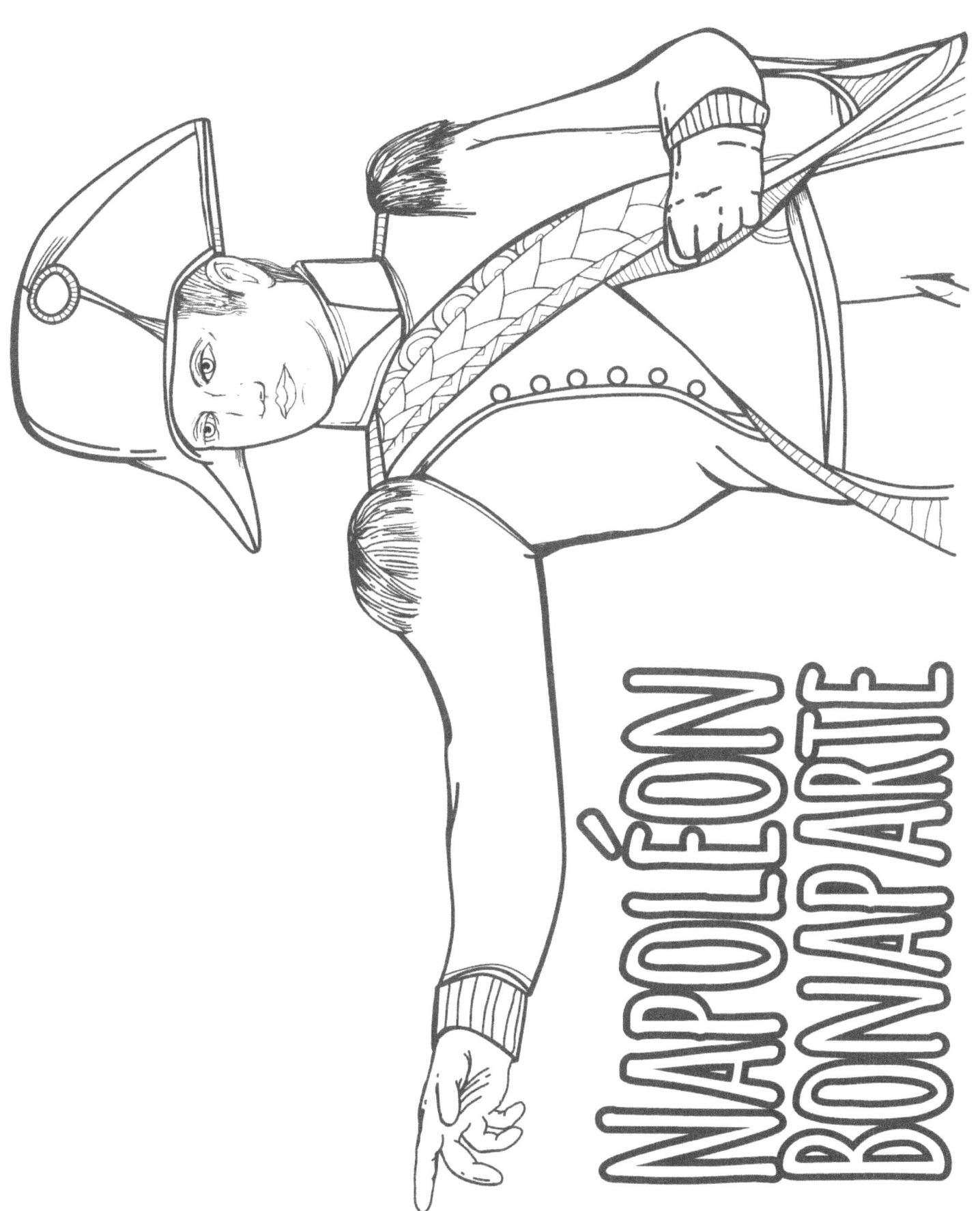

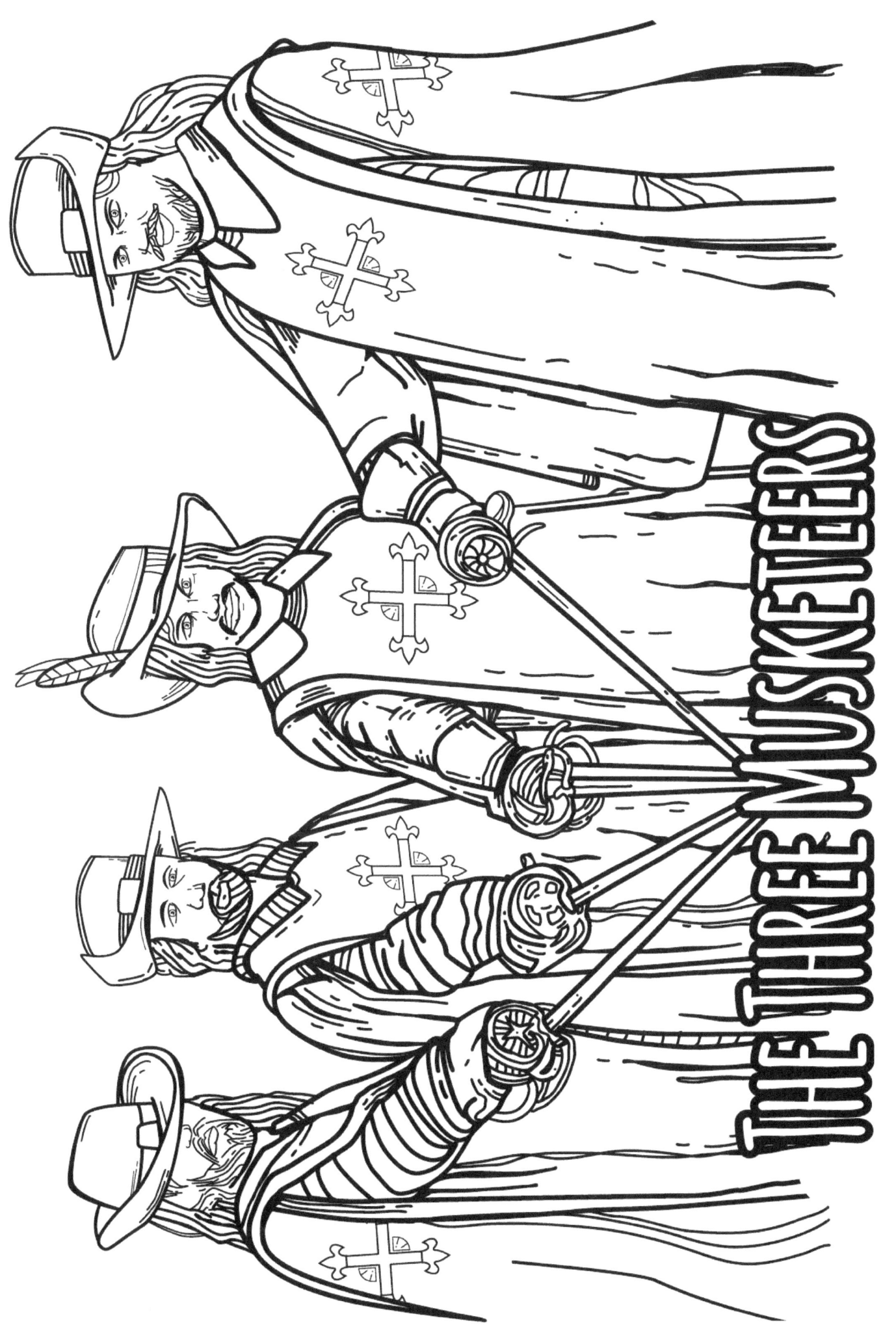

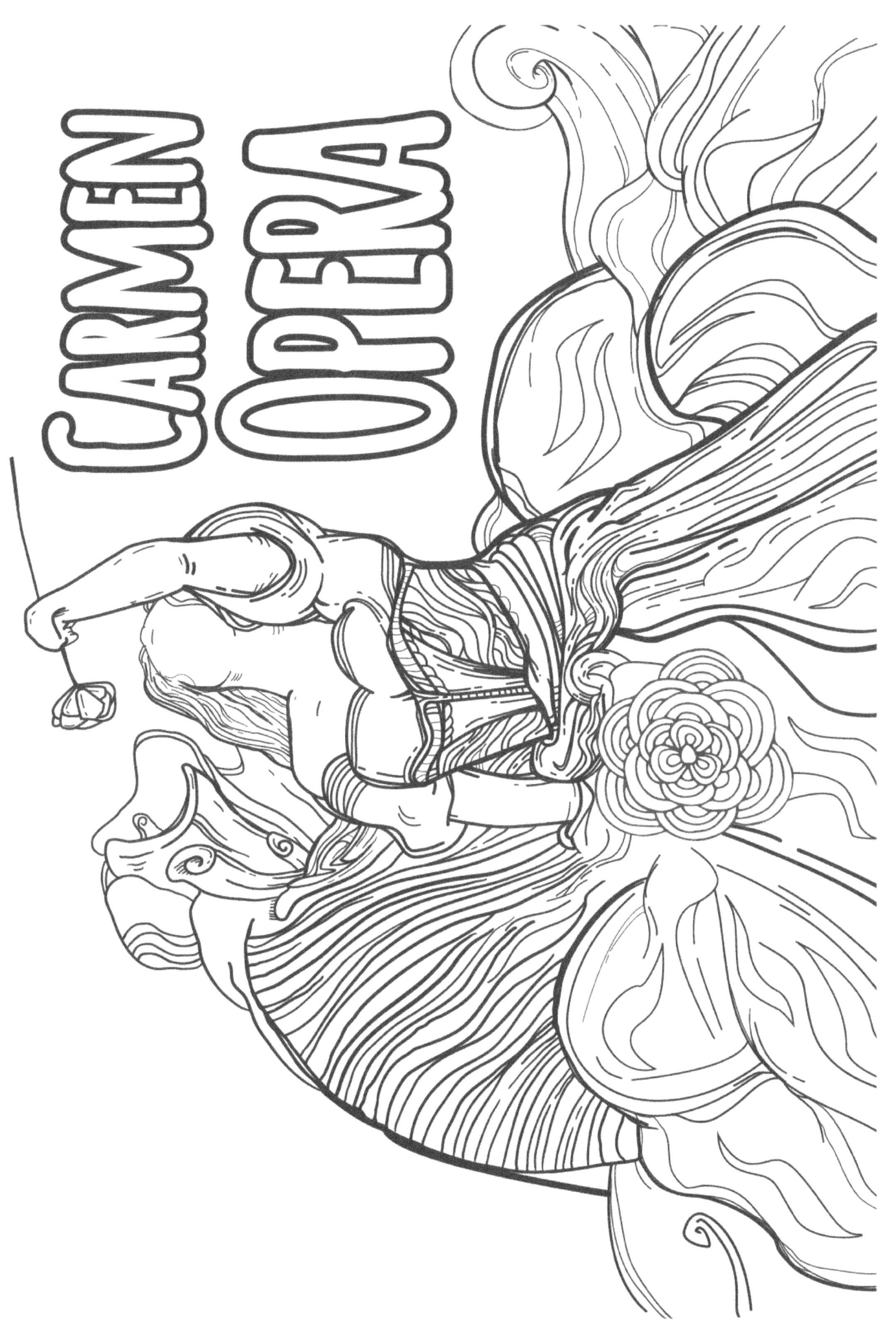

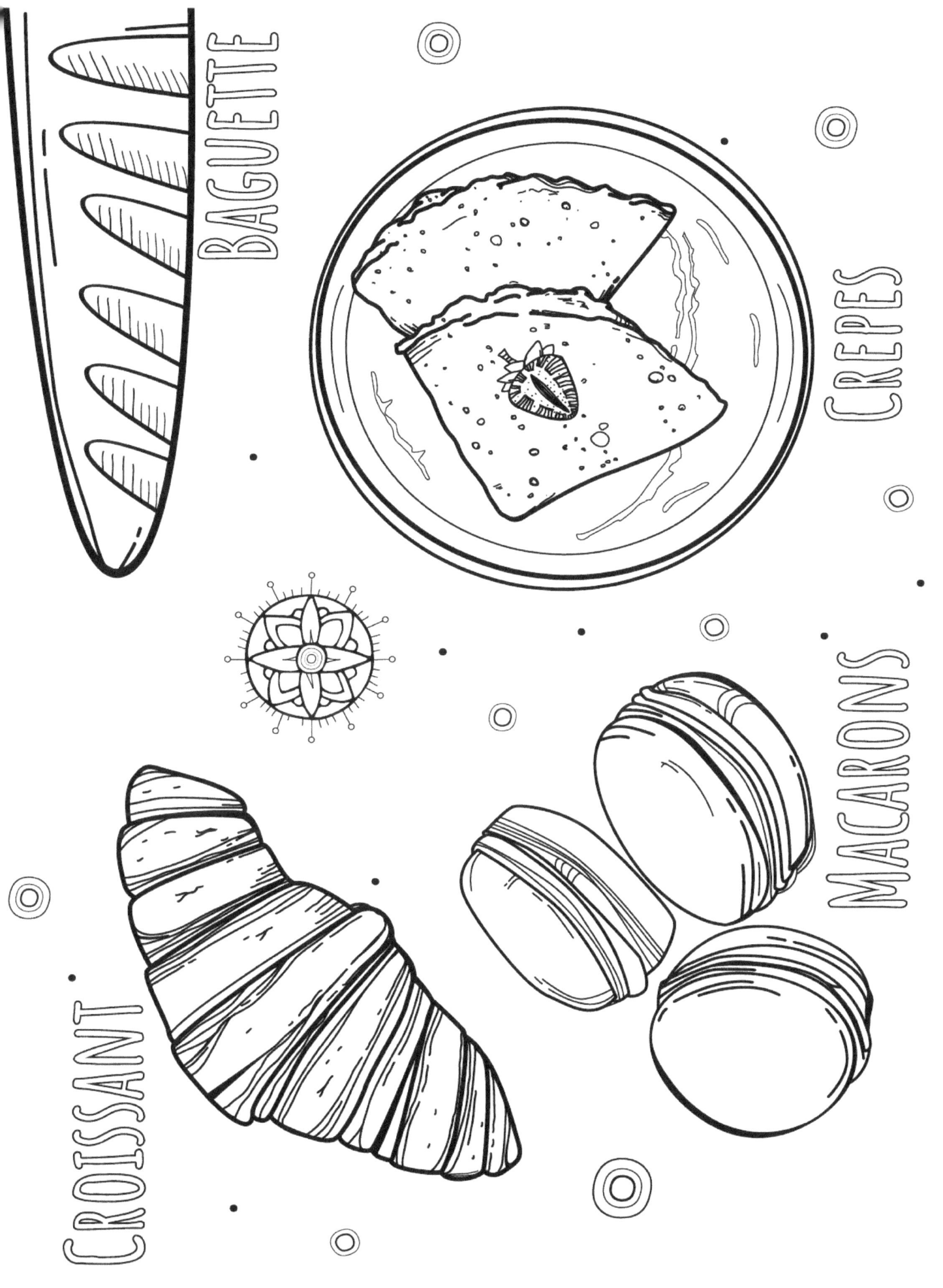

BAGUETTE

CREPES

MACARONS

CROISSANT

CHEESE

CHAMPAGNE

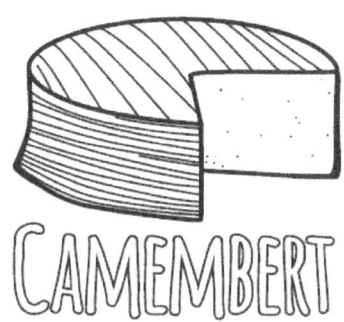

CAMEMBERT

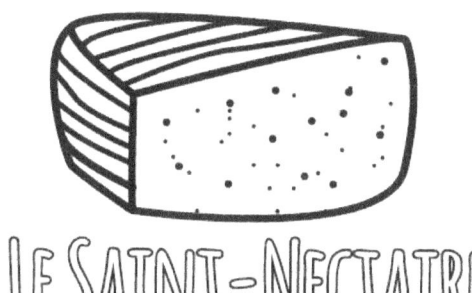

LE SAINT-NECTAIRE

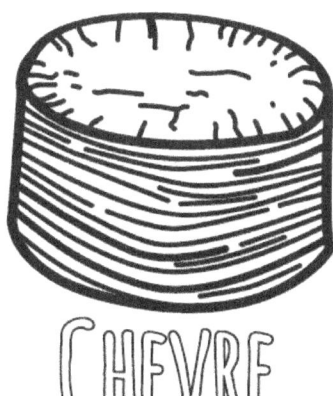

CHEVRE

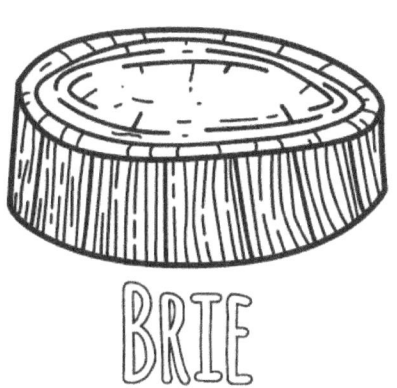

BRIE

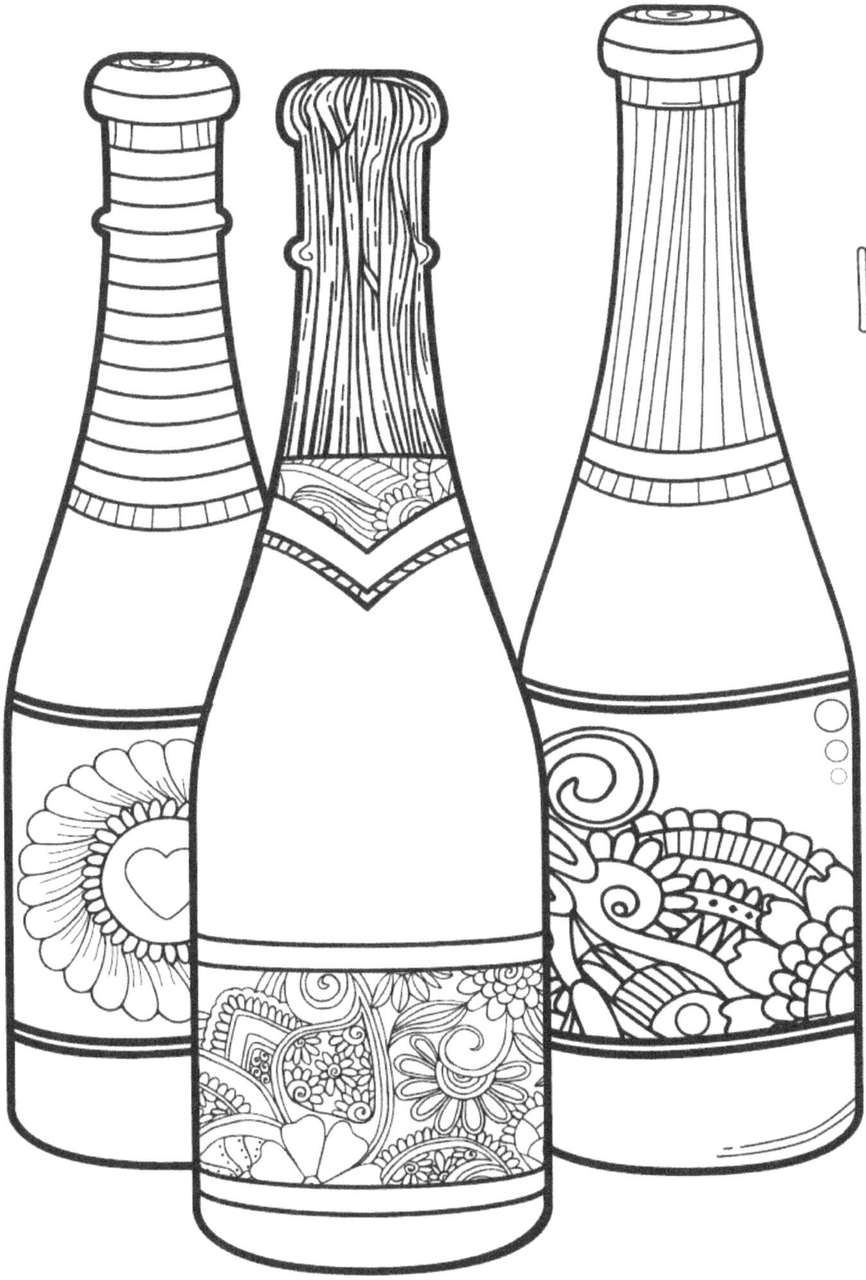

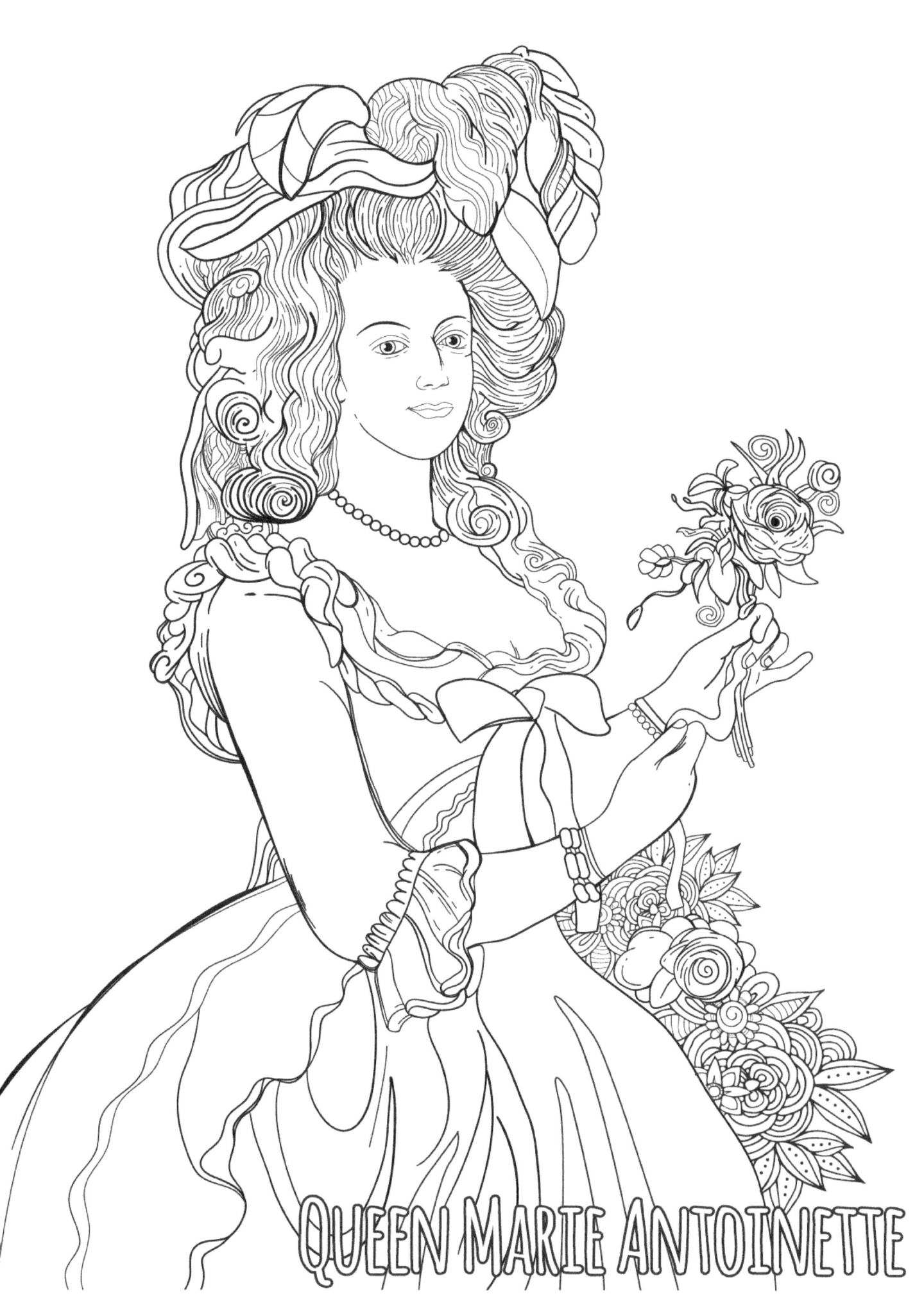

Queen Marie Antoinette

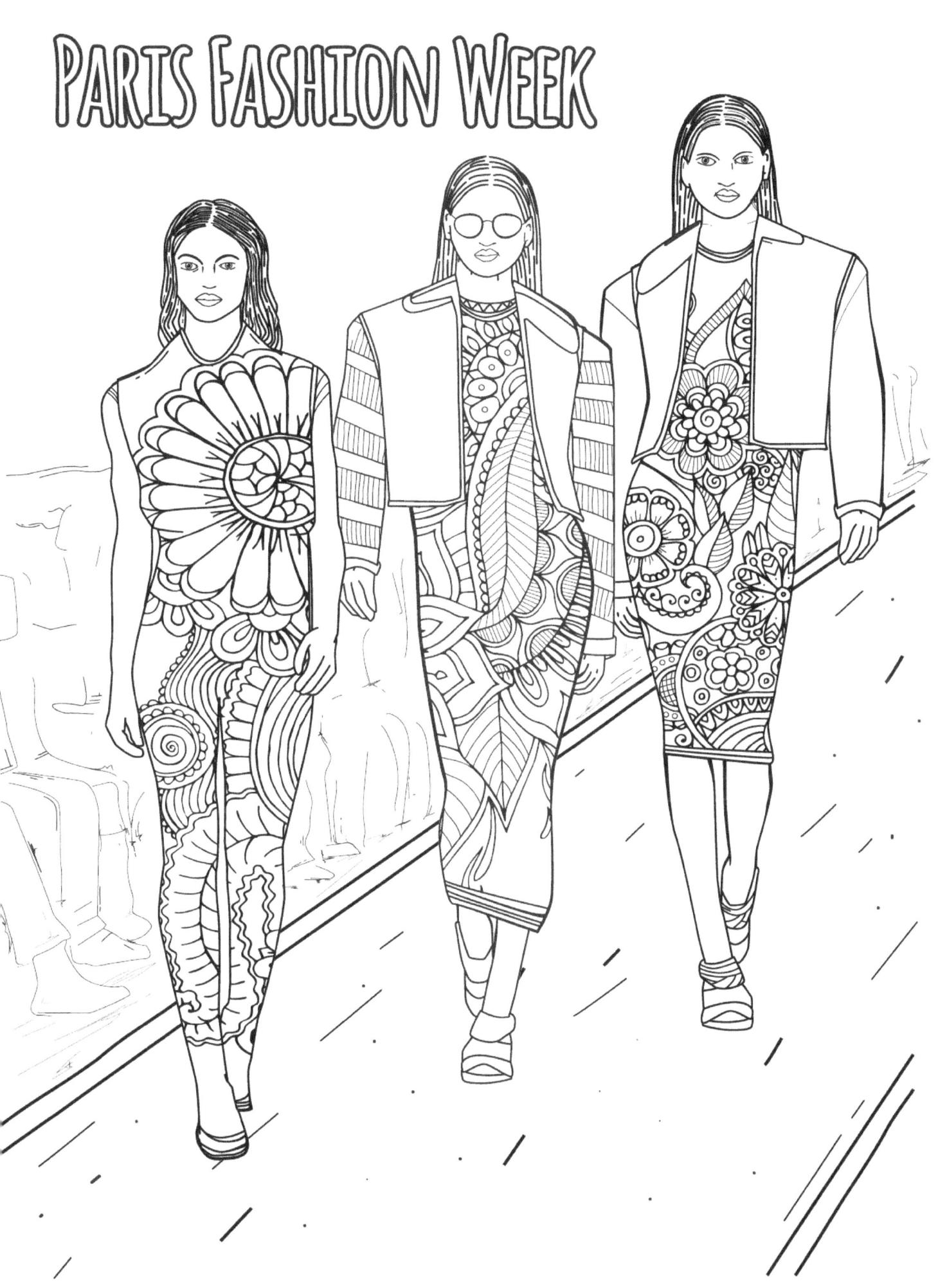

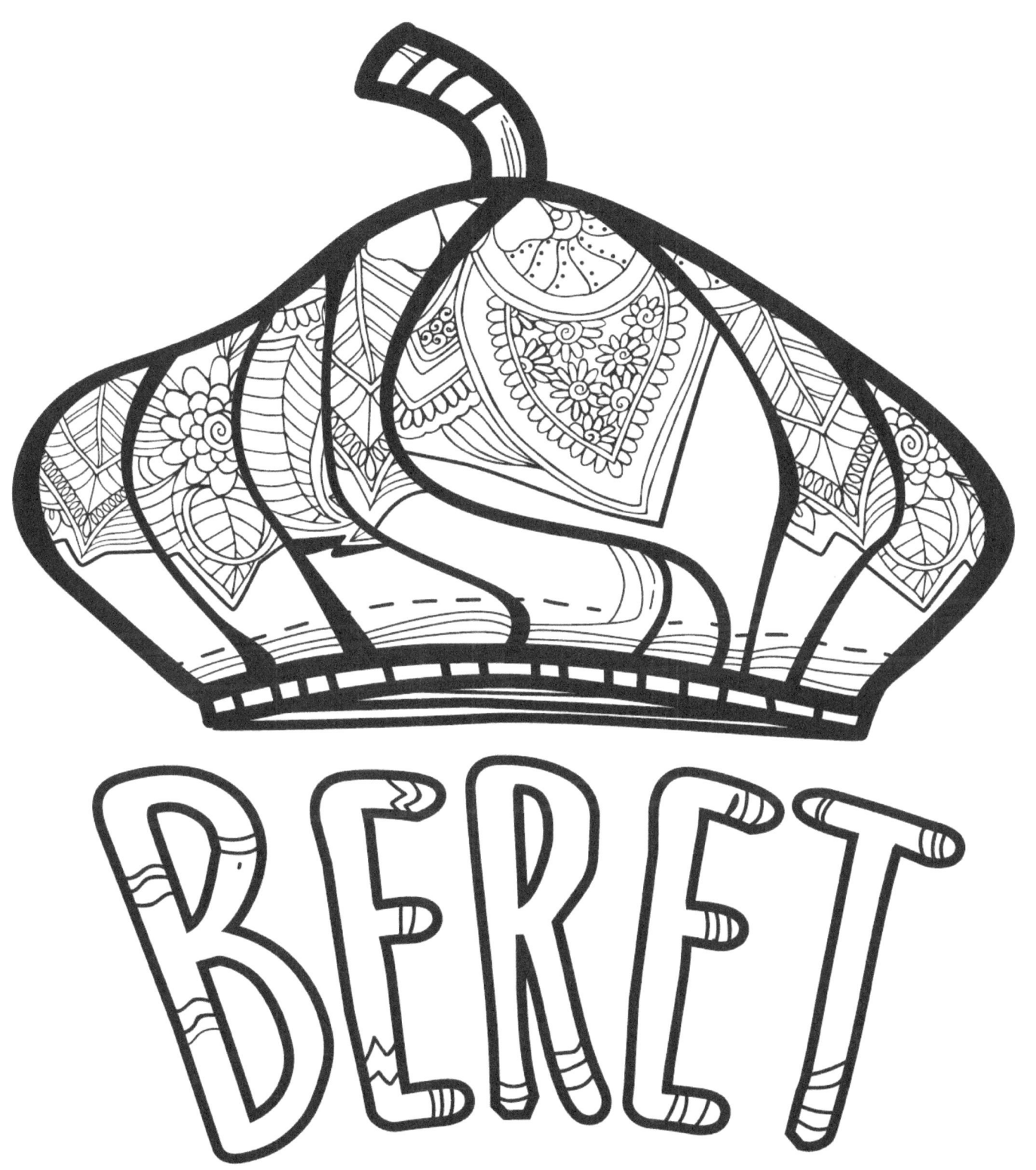

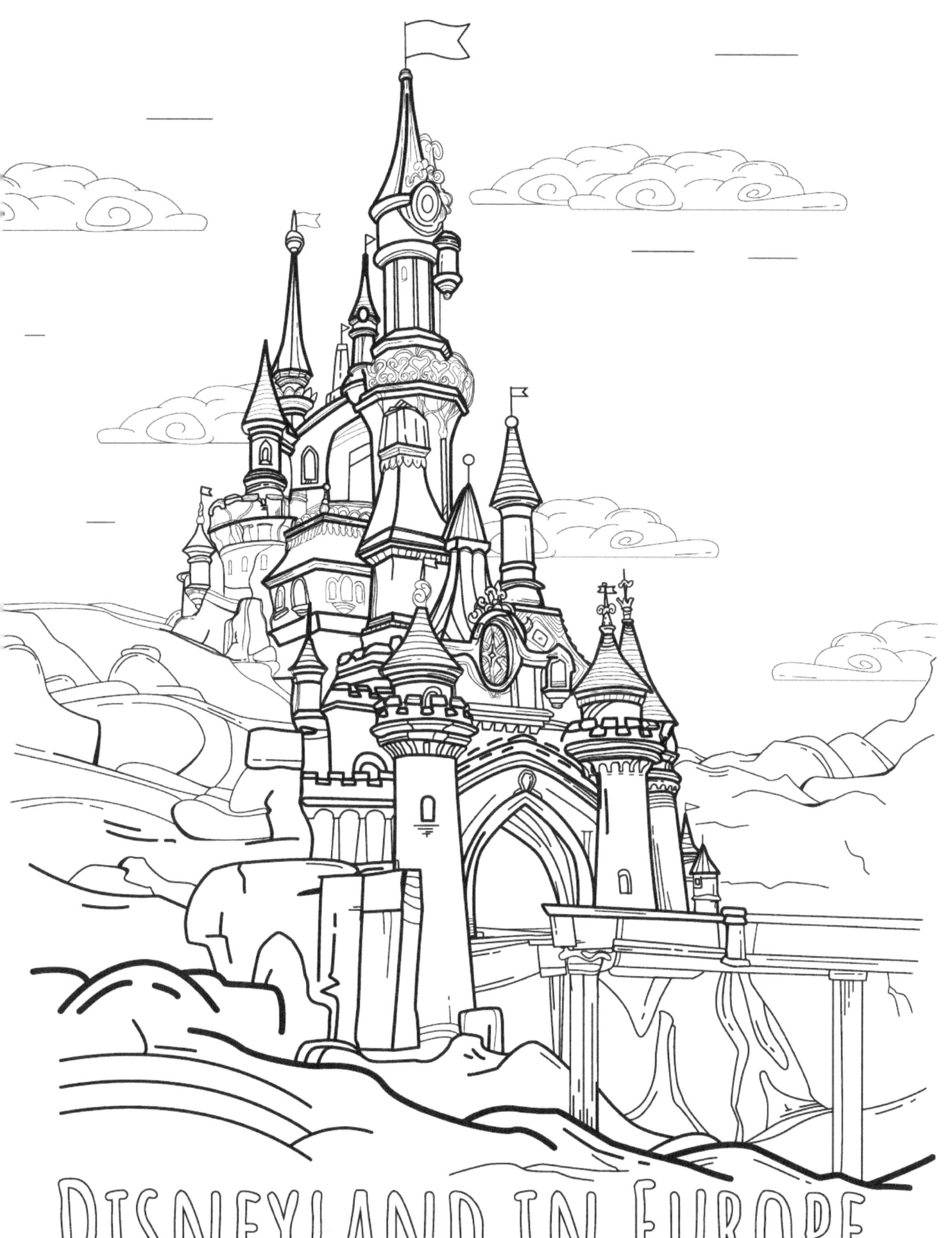

DISNEYLAND IN EUROPE

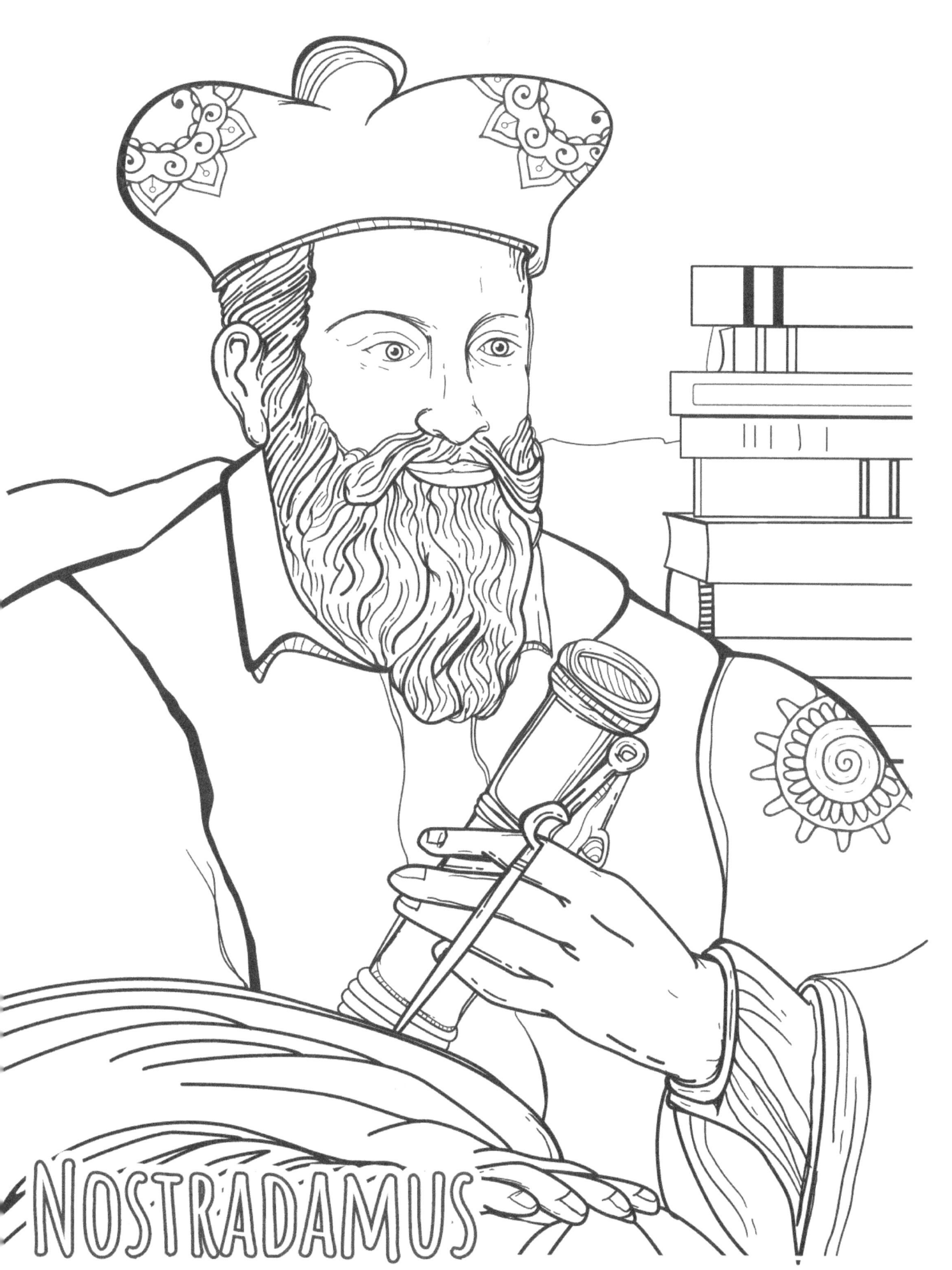

NOSTRADAMUS

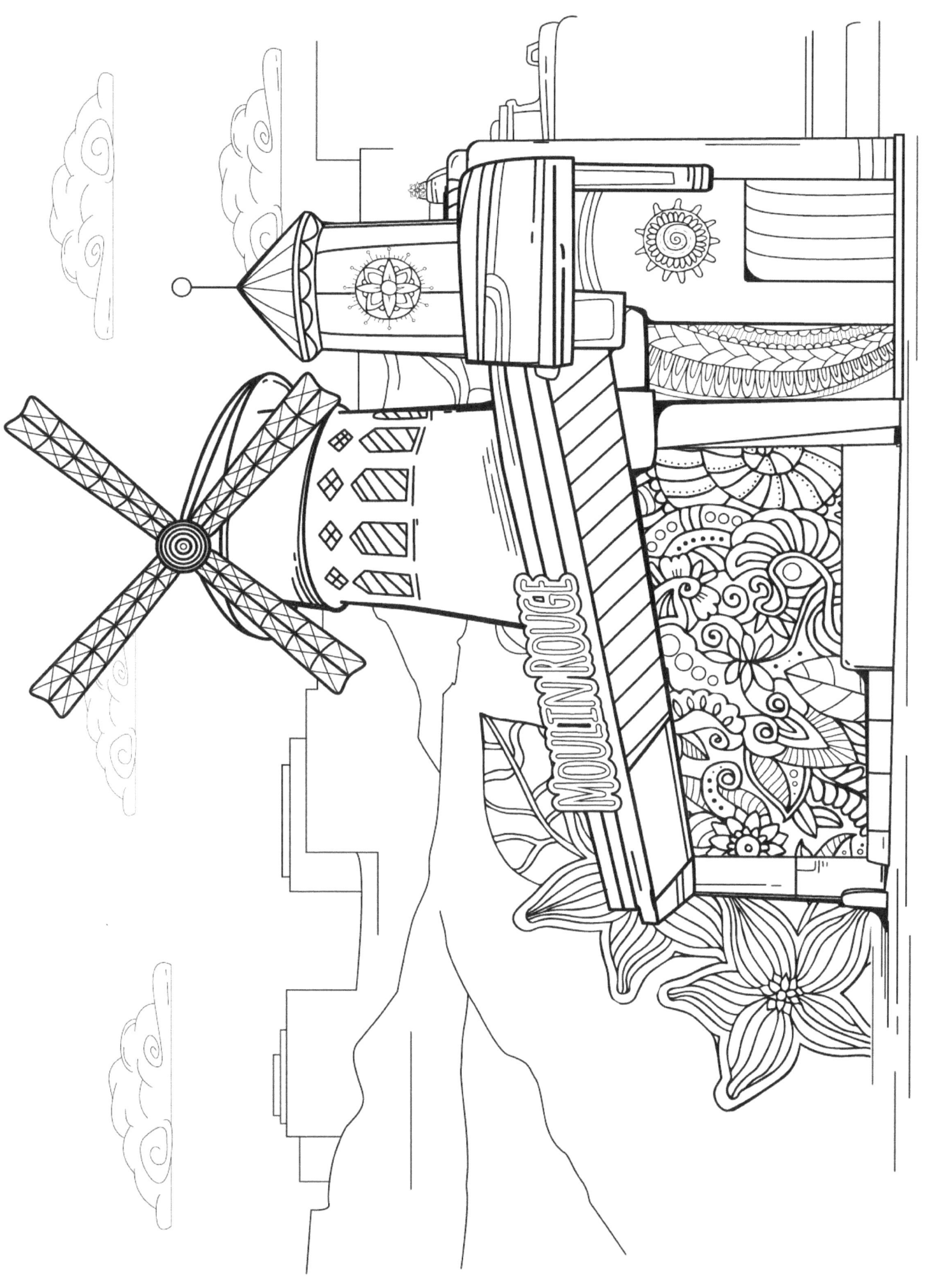

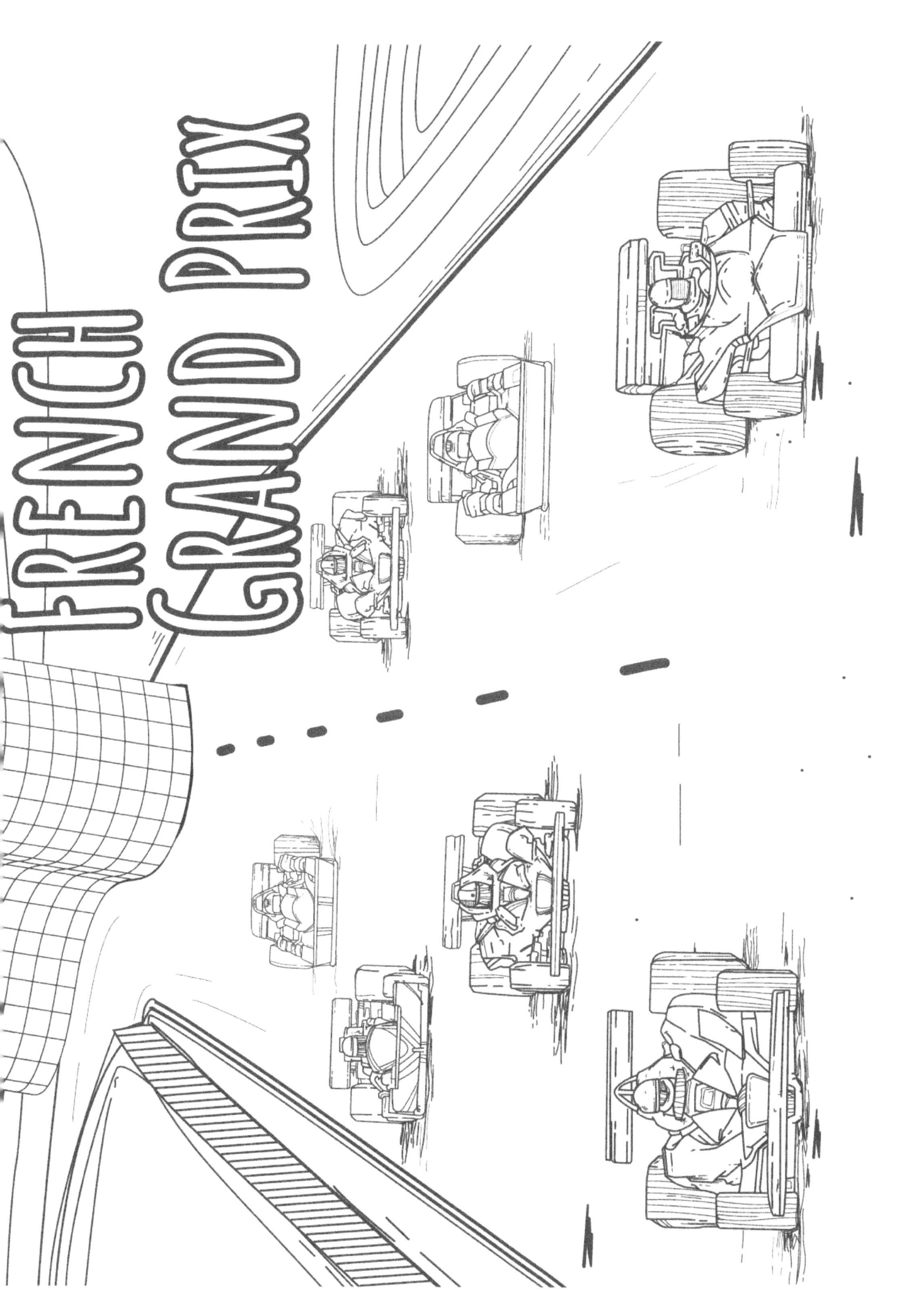

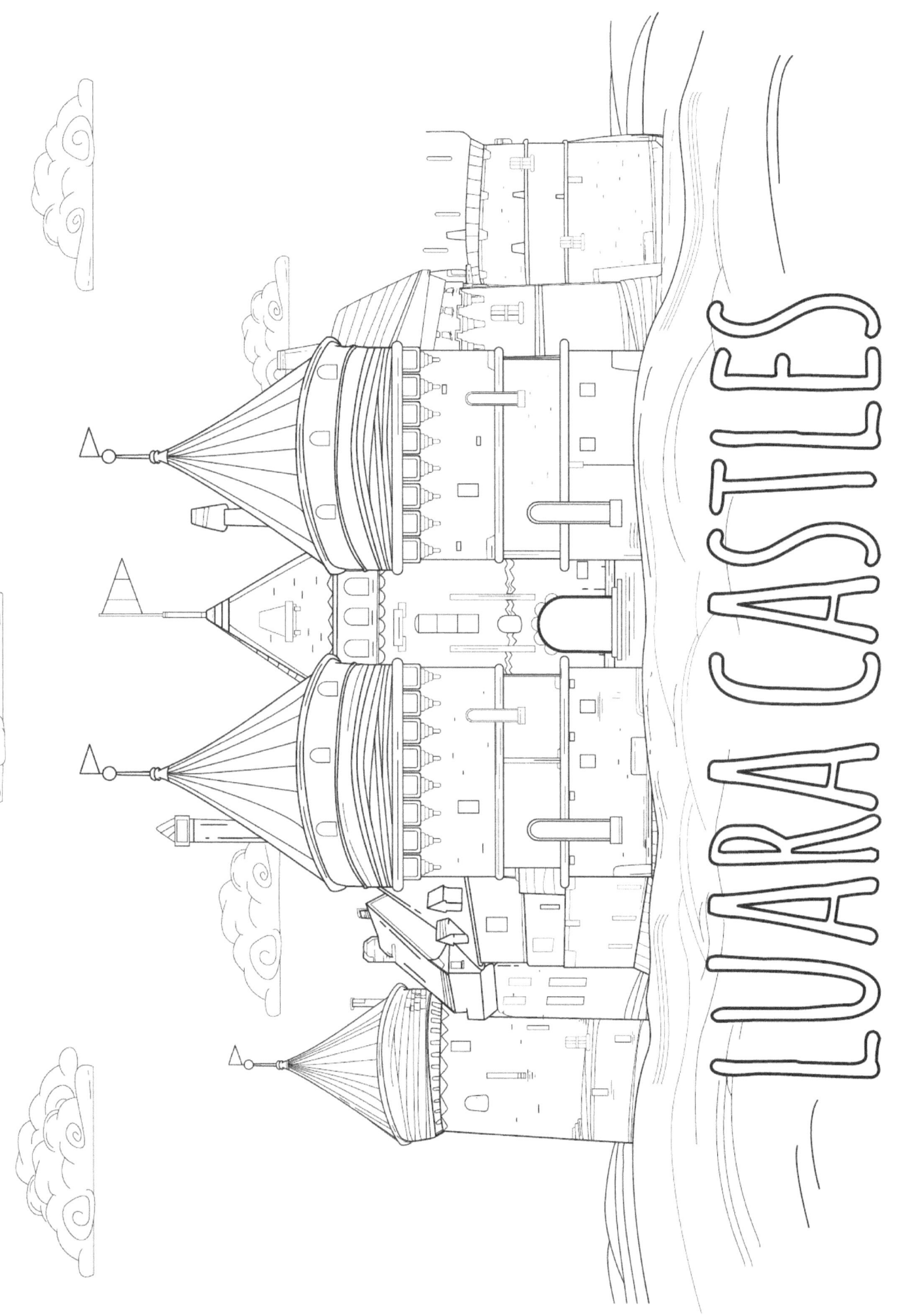

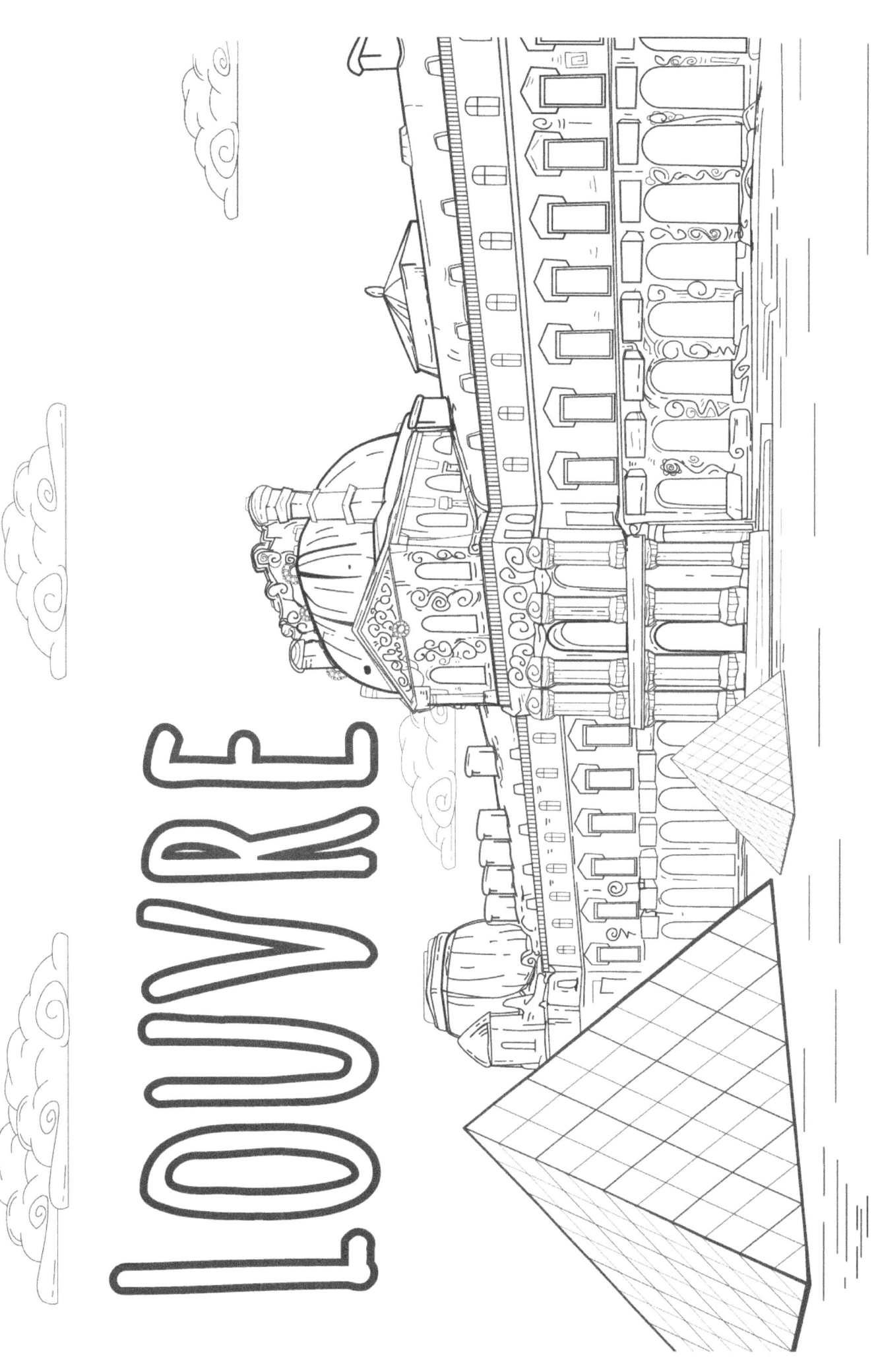

Thank you for purchasing this book.

If you would like to know more about Aryla Publishing Books please visit:-

www.ArylaPublishing.com

Or follow us on
Facebook
Twitter
Instagram
for *free promotions*

@arylapublishing

We would love to know what you think of this book so please leave us a review.

Have a wonderful day

Other Coloring Books from Aryla Publishing

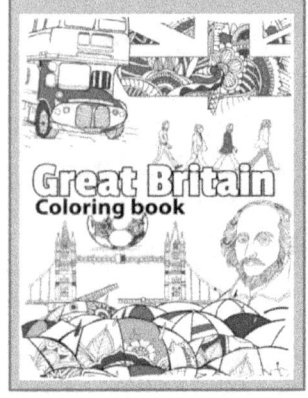
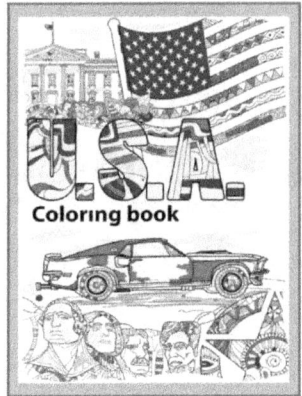
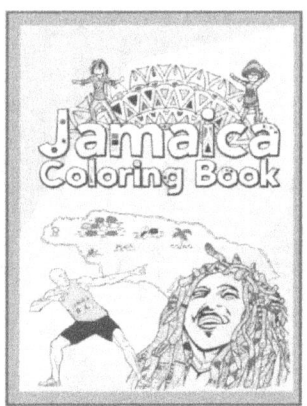
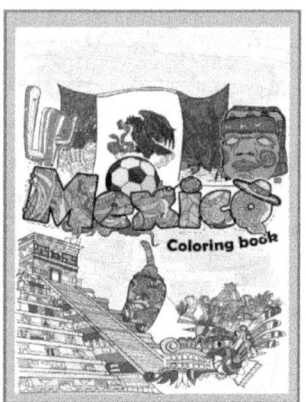

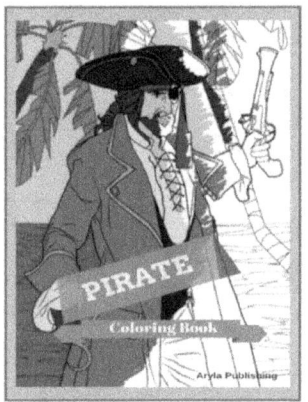
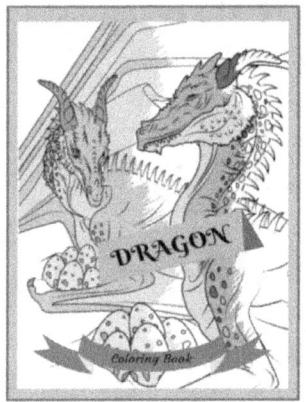
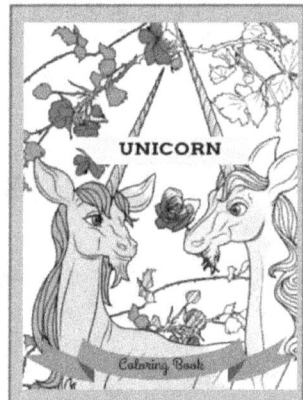
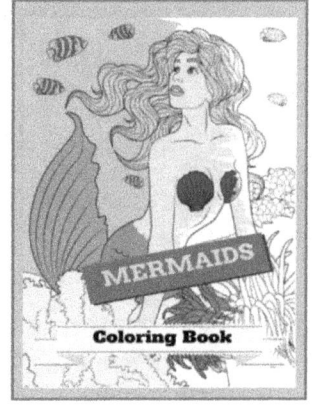

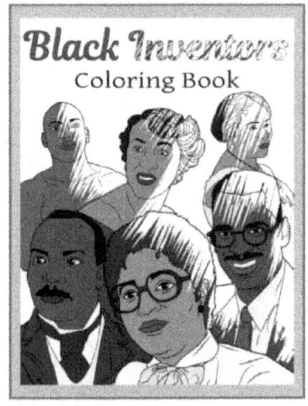
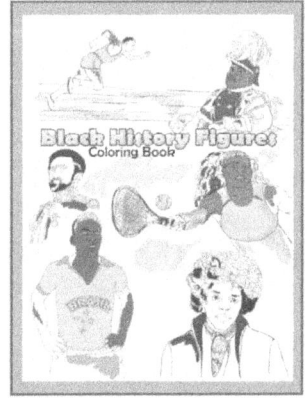
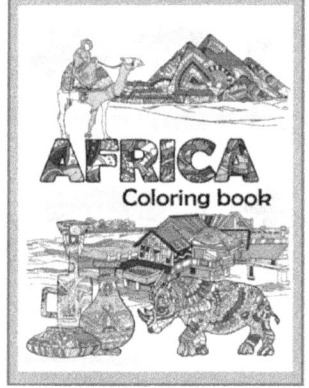
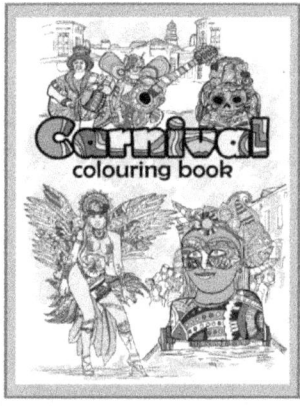

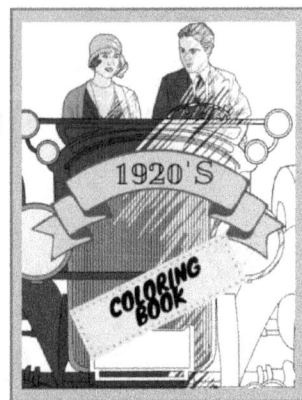
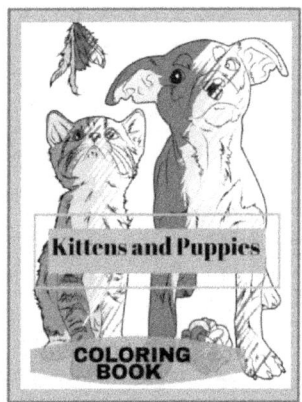
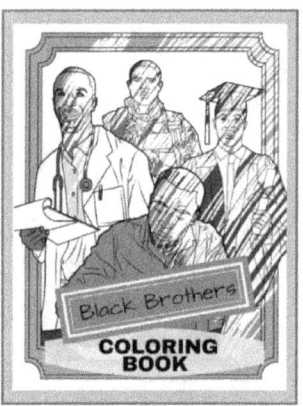
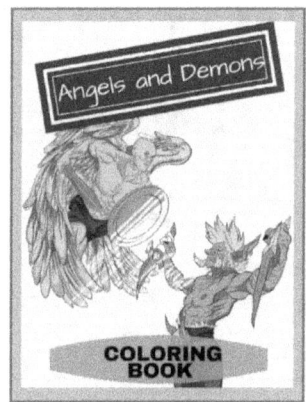

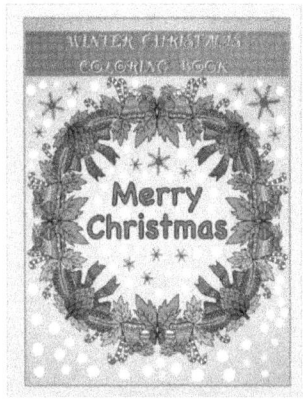
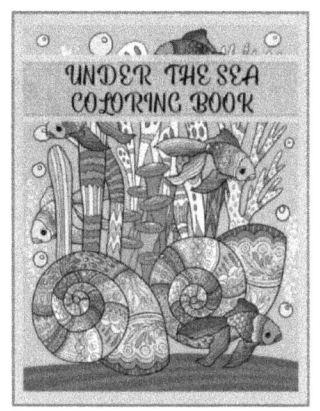
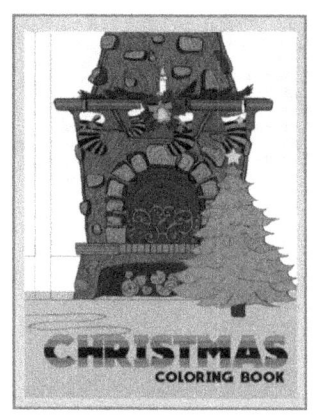
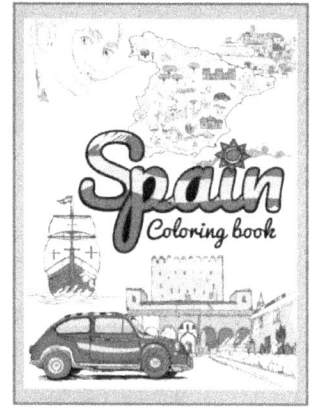
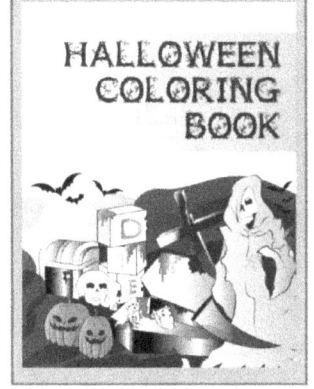
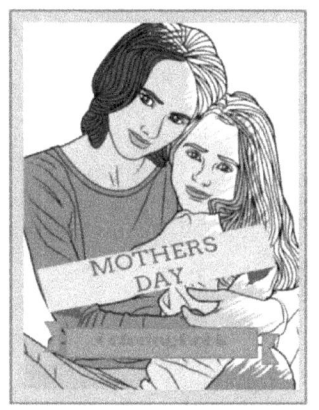
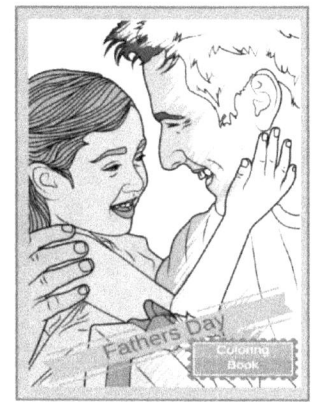
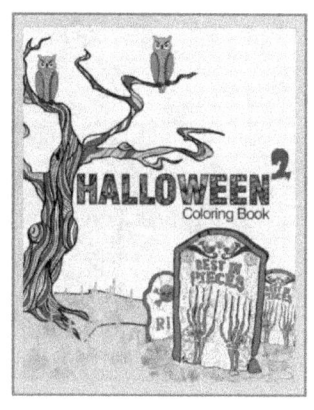
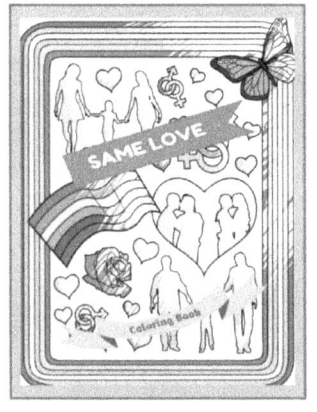
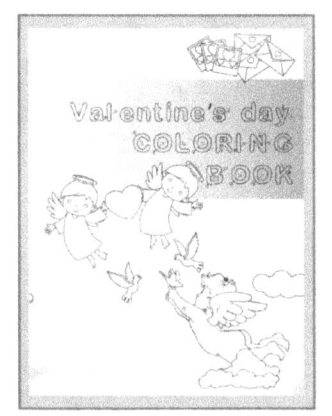
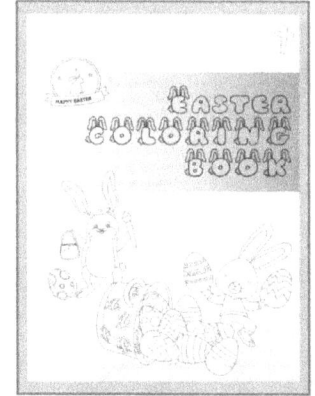
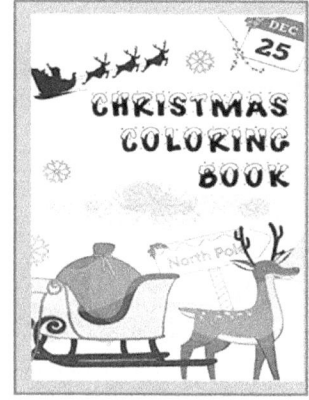
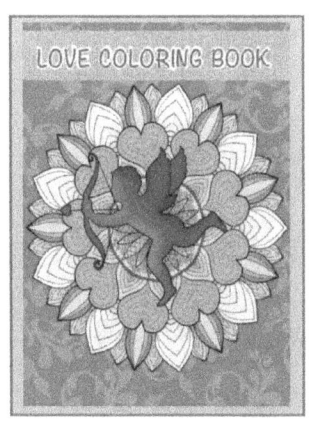
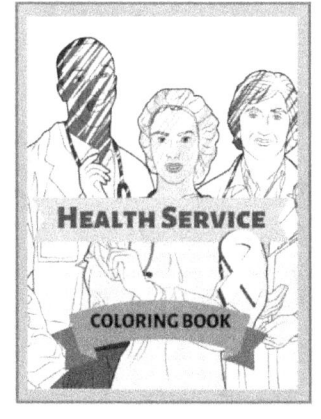
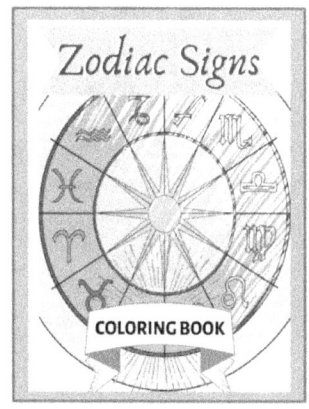
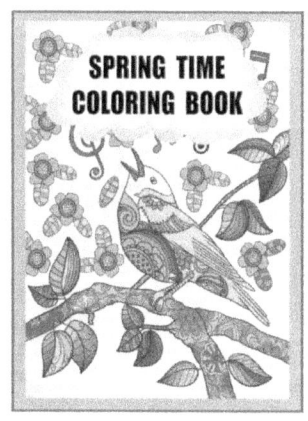

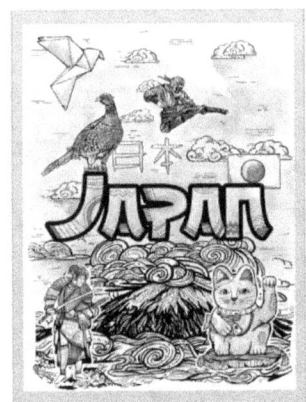
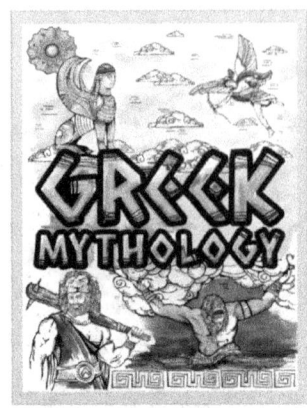
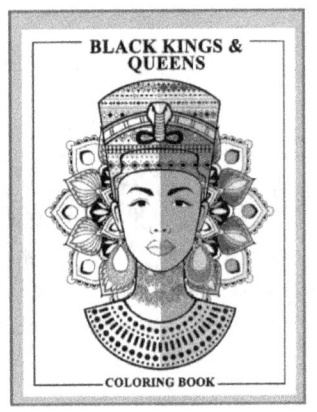
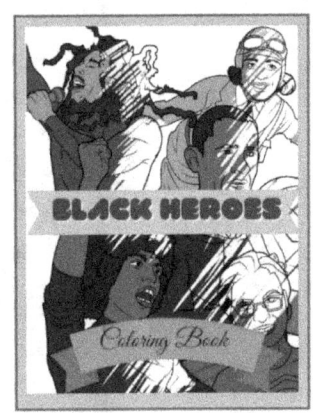
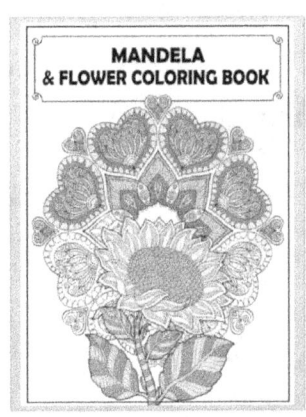
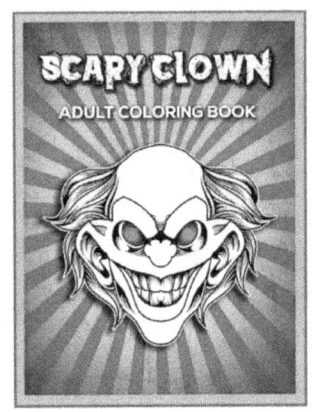
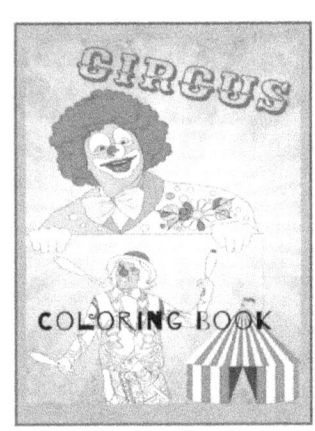
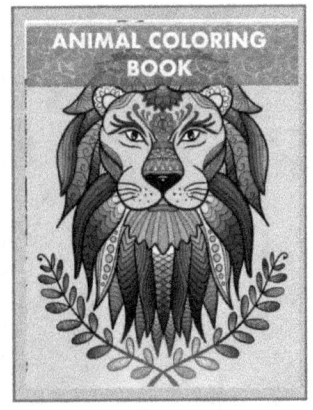
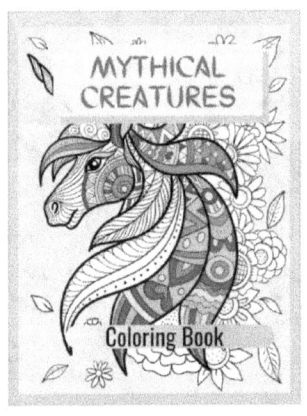
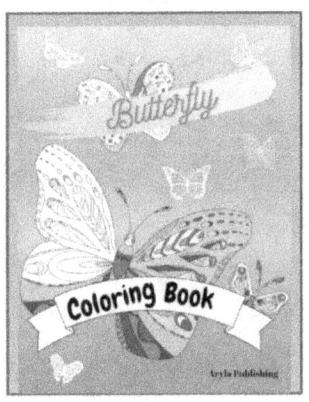

Color In Fun
Kids Books

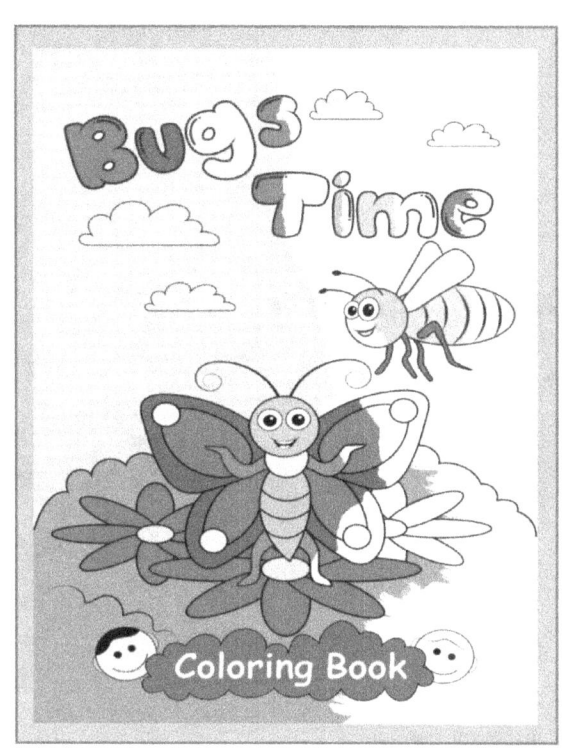

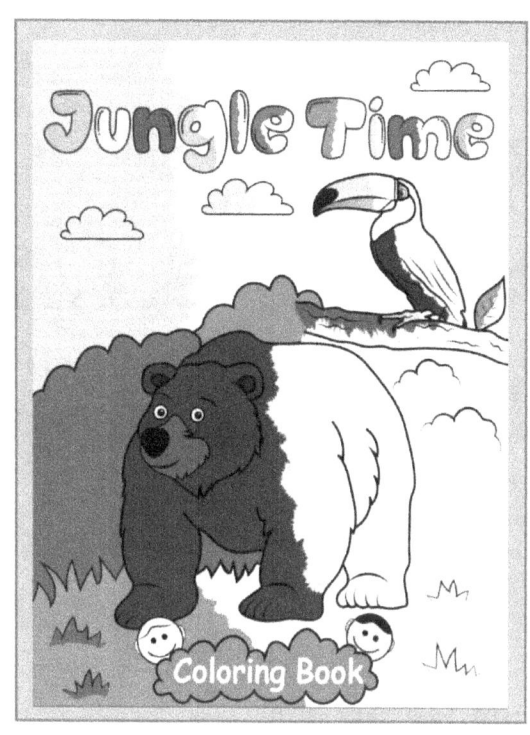

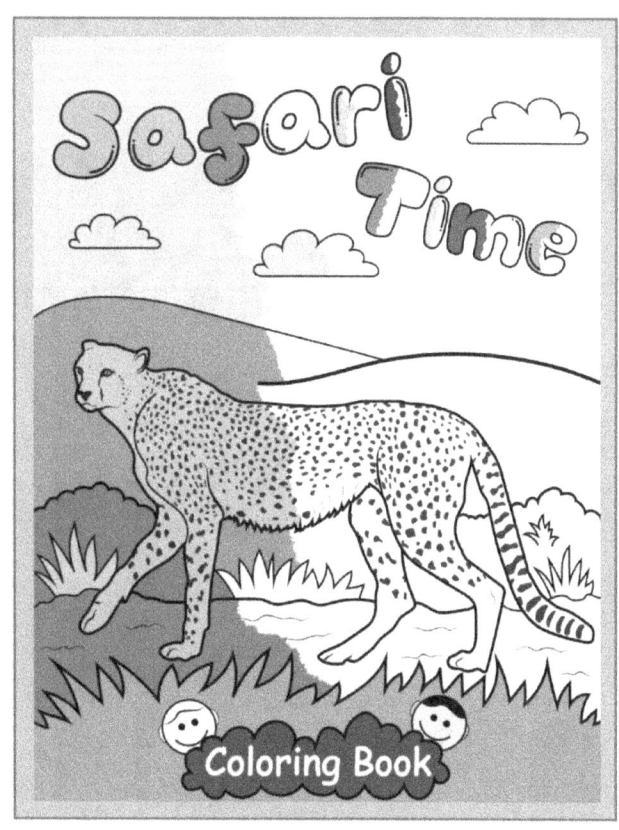

Visit **www.ArylaPublishing.com**
to find out about all new releases.

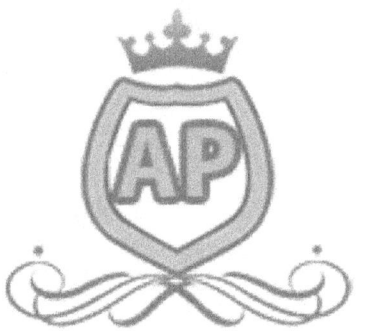

Follow us @arylapublishing on Twitter Instagram & Facebook

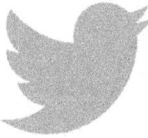  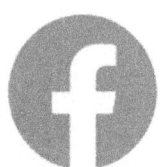

Search for Aryla Publishing on

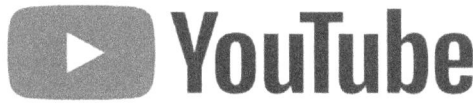

Check out our <u>Book Trailers</u>

<u>*Subscribe*</u> **to keep up to date with new releases!**

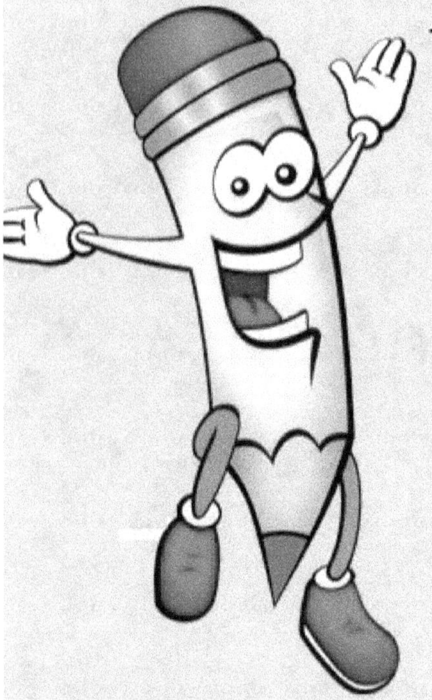

WE WOULD LOVE YOUR FEEDBACK

PLEASE LEAVE REVIEW AT:-

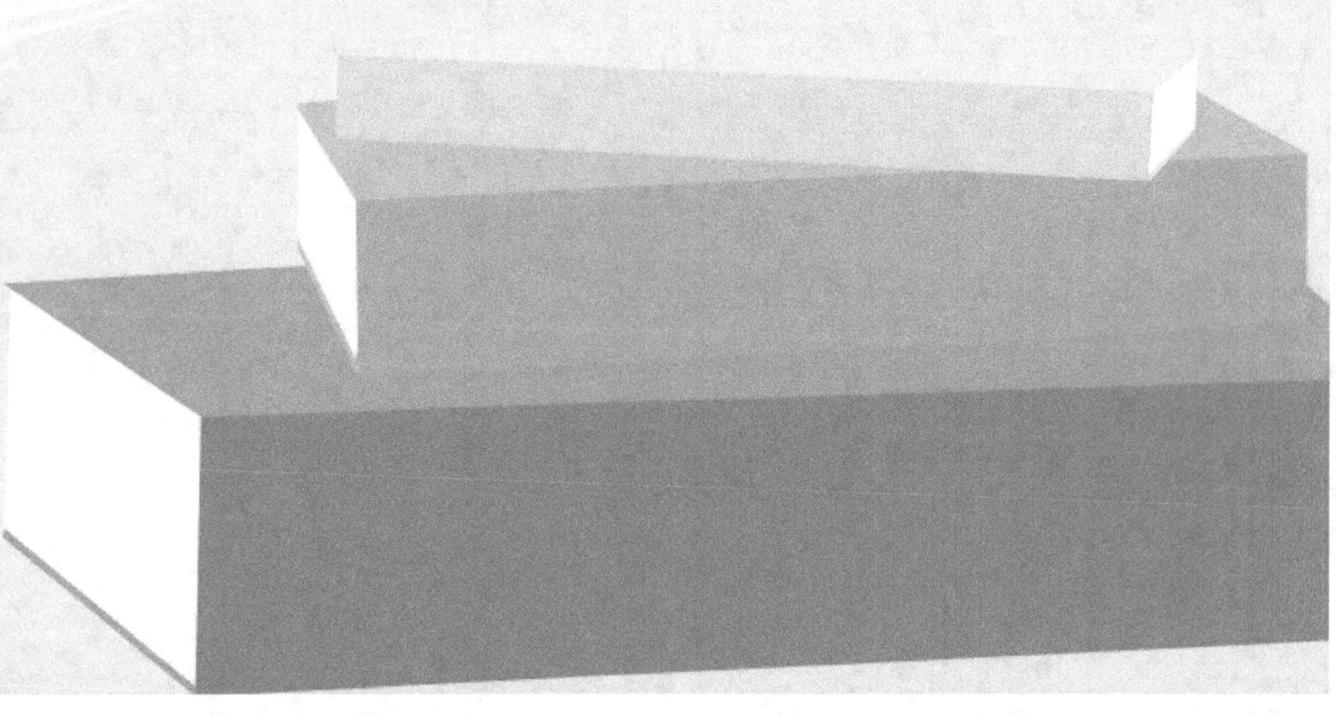

www.ingramcontent.com/pod-product-compliance
Lightning Source LLC
Chambersburg PA
CBHW081744220526
45468CB00008B/2229